Revelations of

PROFOUND LOVE

New Insights
Into the Power of Love
From Near-Death Experiences

Revelations of
PROFOUND LOVE

New Insights
Into the Power of Love
From Near-Death Experiences

Ann Frances Ellis, Ph.D.

Trail of Hope Publishing
Tulsa, Oklahoma

First edition, second printing

Copyright © 2012 by Ann Frances Ellis

All rights reserved under the Pan-American and International Copyright Conventions. This book may not be reproduced, in whole or in part, in any form or by any means electronic or mechanical, including photocopying, recording, or by any information storage and retrieval system now known or hereafter invented, without written permission from the publisher, Trail of Hope Publishing.

Revelations of Profound Love
Cover photo by Socrates | dreamstime.com
Printed in the USA

To order this title, please contact:

Trail of Hope Publishing
at
www.revelationsofprofoundlove.com

Library of Congress Control Number: 2012952859

DEDICATION

I dedicate this book to my beloved father,

Benjamin Franklin Ellis, Jr.

Daddy, you were the best father.
Thank you for your love, attention, and devotion
while you were here on earth
and ever since.

CONTENTS

PREFACE

This book brings a message of hope, a message of love: You are loved more than you can even imagine—now and always.

Here are first-person accounts from ordinary people who had powerful other-worldly experiences, often when they were near death. These people tell of encountering incredible love. They talk about traveling to their true home, in the light, where all is love. They bring back the discoveries they made. These discoveries are for all of us:

§ There truly is no death: only the physical body dies. We are alive and well after we leave our physical bodies. We go to a world of great splendor and love. We don't need to fear death.

§ The true nature of love is much greater than we here on earth can imagine. It is immeasurably powerful. It is the substance from which all creation is formed. Love is the energy, vibration, and force of the universe.

§ There are many qualities of this higher love. It is unconditional—nothing can diminish or destroy it. In the world of love and light, there is neither judgment nor exclusion. There is peace, all knowledge, compassion, tolerance, and joy.

§ This love radiates from many sources. The ultimate source of the love is The One, God, Creator—there are many names. Even the light itself exudes this love. Jesus and other light beings emanate this love as well.

§ All creation is connected in love and is part of the One. Love is our essence and at the core of our being. No one has ever been alone or ever will be.

§ Every life on earth has a purpose, chosen before coming here. The ultimate purpose of life is love—to learn about love in all its forms and to express it. There is a higher purpose for everything that happens, even suffering, although it may not be clear to us at the time. We may choose to return to earth as many times as we wish to learn more about love.

§ In life, the only thing that matters is love. What is important during our stay on earth is treating everyone with love and kindness, living life fully, and choosing higher thoughts, emotions, and vibrations. Everything we have done with love is of value; all else is dissolved when we leave earth. The love we know on earth will never end, and we will be with our loved ones forever.

These discoveries reveal the power of love. I now believe this love is here for all of us, in this world as well as the next, and that the understandings and insights these people brought back can enhance our lives and mitigate our deaths.

These accounts of near-death experiences of profound love have touched my heart, and I hope they touch yours as well. I know some of these concepts can be difficult, and it took me a long time to believe them all. Be gentle with yourself, if this is the first time you have heard some of these things. Look to your own inner guidance for your own truth. We are each in the perfect place for us right now.

It is my hope that these messages of love will be a blessing to you, as they have been to me.

Chapter One

Introduction

MY SEARCH TO UNDERSTAND LOVE

When I was two years old, something mysterious happened to me that set into motion a lifetime of seeking. Although I didn't remember this event until recently, it laid the foundation for my search to understand love, the other side, and near-death experiences. This is what I remember of that event:

Daddy is wading into the Potomac River with me in his arms, showing me the churning water of the rapids. Oh, no! What happened? My hands are slipping off his bare shoulder! I can't hold on! Now water is tossing me all around.

Suddenly, I am standing in a bright room. I am about the size of a six-year-old girl. A beautiful lady is seated to my left. She looks like a princess with her blond hair and long flowing gown. I talk to her and she listens with compassion and respect. I tell her it is harder down there than I remembered.

Then I realize Daddy will be devastated if I don't go back. I decide to return, for him. Now I am soaring above a moving ambulance. Now I'm waking up in a hospital bed. I look around for Mommy and Daddy, but nobody's here. Suddenly, the door flings open and Mommy and Daddy rush in. They are so happy and excited to see me alive! I begin to sob. I feel so loved!

Although my conscious memory of this experience faded as I grew older and did not return for many years, I now believe it affected me deeply. It changed me from a happy-go-lucky little girl to one who understood things beyond her years. I seemed to know how people were feeling, especially those who were hurting, and I often viewed things differently from the way other people did. Even when my father died of cancer when I was seven, I somehow felt comforted and knew everything was all right. Throughout my life, though I worked nearly three decades as a scientist, I always knew there was "something more" than our ordinary reality.

Then, when I was thirty-two, another mysterious experience reminded me of who I am and revealed to me the power of God's love. During an early-morning communion service, I was praying silently in a tiny chapel as the priest was preparing the bread and wine. While I was staring at the lit candle that had been placed on the altar, my gaze was drawn toward the ceiling. Suddenly a strange river of energy began flowing into me from a small bright window there, flooding me with what I could only describe as immense love. It filled my body from my toes to the top of my head. It felt fantastic. I knew I was loved, and I could feel my heart opening and enlarging. When I could hold no more, the flow of love stopped as suddenly as it had begun, leaving my heart overflowing. I sat wondering what had happened to me and thought to myself, *"All I know for sure is that something came from outside of me into me."* The feeling of overwhelming love persisted through the remainder of the service, but I left without mentioning it to anyone.

While driving to work from the chapel that morning, I felt love for everyone and everything my gaze took in. I saw a lady waiting at the bus stop and felt love going out of me to her. I watched a squirrel run up a tree and felt great love for it. I looked around as though seeing familiar landmarks for the first time. As I drove down the parkway, the trees and leaves and the sunlight dancing on them enchanted me even more than usual.

When I got to work, I still felt enchanted, but I couldn't bask in that feeling too long when there was work to be done. But when I drove home after work, I again felt that energy and love flood into me, especially when I shifted my gaze upward toward the sky for a moment. I also noticed that colors were more vivid than usual and the beauty of all nature was enhanced through my new vision. I felt very close to God and began talking to God whenever I was alone, especially while I was driving, and basking in that love each time.

The overpowering sense of love and aliveness lasted for months. For many years, I could get that feeling back, with somewhat diminishing power. Eventually I began taking it for granted, and one day I found I had lost my ability to get it back.

I kept this experience to myself. I didn't understand it and didn't know how to talk about it. I thought I was the only one this had ever happened to.

But then, four years later, I found out I wasn't the only person who had experienced something beyond ordinary reality. A friend had invited me to a lecture by Elisabeth Kübler-Ross, a medical doctor known for her pioneering work in the field of death and dying. Dr. Kübler-Ross, a tiny woman who spoke with a heavy accent, gave vivid descriptions of dying patients who talked about seeing their deceased loved ones coming for them. She seemed to be saying that our loved ones survive death. These were things I had never heard anyone talk about before. Without even thinking about it, I spontaneously said to my friend, "I know that's true." Somehow, I spoke from a place in my heart where I knew of this reality.

When I got home from her lecture, I listened to her tape over and over and it fed my soul. My heart could tap into the reality her patients had told her about. Later, when I came across Raymond Moody's book, *Life After Life,*[1] I learned about additional aspects of this reality. I was captivated by the stories he quoted from people who had died and gone into that greater reality before returning later to their bodies. He called this type of visit to another world a "near-death experience," or "NDE" for short. I devoured every word he quoted from the "near-death experiencers" describing their travels and encounters in the world beyond death. And I read every book that came along about near-death experiences. As I slowly assimilated what I was learning about life after death, my worldview had to change to keep up with it.

Several years later, I was diagnosed with cancer and had to confront my own mortality. When I phoned my grown son to tell him about my diagnosis and upcoming surgery, some more surprising words came out of my mouth. I heard myself saying, "I want to help people deal with death and dying, as Elisabeth Kübler-Ross has." As I said this, I saw a picture in my mind of an open book. Kübler-Ross's groundbreaking book, *On Death and Dying,*[2] has helped many people understand that dying is a natural process with five basic phases, and that it ought to be discussed openly. I knew at that moment that I, too, would someday write a book to help others cope with death.

After my successful cancer surgery I felt an urgency to immediately begin supporting others who were facing their own mortality. So I contacted the Cancer Society to volunteer with a cancer support group and began volunteering with a local hospice as well. I also contacted the city hospital, and their chaplain invited me to serve as a lay on-call night minister. This was another volunteer position, but one where I could share with patients and families my understanding of God's love and of life after death.

I especially enjoyed volunteering as a night minister, so within a few years, I enrolled part-time in a Master of Divinity program to prepare to serve as a professional chaplain. After being offered the opportunity of early retirement from my first profession as a computer network manager, I completed my seminary studies and worked as a hospice chaplain for several years.

I MEET MY FIRST NEAR-DEATH EXPERIENCERS

In 1994, a few years before I retired, I discovered the International Association for Near-Death Studies (IANDS)[3] and jumped at the opportunity to join. I attended their next annual conference and was thrilled to meet so many people like me. I felt right at home, and I was deeply touched when I listened to near-death experiencers who choked up while sharing their stories. I sensed their sincerity and how hard it was for them to share their sacred encounters. I was honored to hear their stories and I had so many questions for them. I wanted to learn everything they knew about the other side, and especially about the love they encountered there.

I returned to IANDS conferences year after year to renew the spiritual connection I felt there. After a while I noticed that many researchers who presented their findings seemed to avoid the significance of the love reported by so many near-death experiencers. Although many of the quotations they used in their books referred to love on the other side, their conclusions seemed to avoid topics like love, purpose, and meaning, and they often simply grouped love in with other emotions and feelings.[4] Based on my experience of love pouring into me, I felt there was much more to know about love than had been acknowledged.

An opportunity for me to research and write about love became available several years after I began working as a hospice chaplain. Over a period of a few months, I had met several interesting women who had all graduated from the same small seminary in Oklahoma. I wanted to know more about it and went there to find out what it was like. I was impressed with its quiet, natural setting and sensitive advisors, so I enrolled in their doctoral program with the goal of doing research and writing about love.

After beginning my studies, I felt guided to write specifically about the continuity of love beyond death. I knew that near-death experiences demonstrated this. Later, when it was time to start work on my dissertation, I chose to research near-death experiences to find out what more I could learn about that amazing love from them. I entitled my proposed dissertation *Profound Love as Revealed by Near-Death Experiences.*

SEARCHING FOR THE LOVE IN NEAR-DEATH ACCOUNTS

To research the love encountered during near-death experiences, I wanted to study as many accounts as possible, and I turned to IANDS for help. After approving me as an authorized researcher, IANDS provided me with 478 narratives voluntarily submitted to their most recent "NDE Archives." These narratives had been sent to IANDS over several years from a great variety of individuals. They were from many countries and from people in all walks of life, with or without a religious background.

Each person who contributed their account to IANDS had been asked to complete a questionnaire about themselves and their experience and to approve publication of their account. To protect the privacy of contributors, IANDS assigned a pseudonym and a record number to each narrative. I was provided only the accounts whose authors had approved them for research and for publication. [5]

Reading that many accounts was, in itself, a life-changing experience. Each heartfelt account had a profound impact on me. I could not stop reading, and I couldn't skim even one of them. No two were alike. Each contained details that appeared nowhere else. However, there were sufficient recurring elements for me to believe they were describing the same reality beyond earthly existence. Some accounts were only a few sentences long and some were many pages, but I sensed the same integrity, sincerity, and humility in them that I felt when people shared their stories at IANDS conferences.

Not all of the experiences occurred during illness or near death. About a sixth were "mystical" experiences that happened during meditation or emotional crisis. These are called near-death-like experiences (NDLEs) because they have many elements in common with near-death experiences. Some of those who had near-death-like experiences traveled out of their bodies, through a tunnel, and into the light, while others received transcendent knowledge and/or love without leaving their bodies. These experiences were every bit as profound as those that occurred near death, and they contributed significantly to my understanding of love.

Every one of the accounts represents the courage and generosity of an individual who was willing to reveal in writing, often for the first time, something intensely personal. Although I don't use the real names of any writers I didn't contact personally, their stories are real, and I am deeply indebted to those who shared. Many experiencers said in their accounts that it was impossible to adequately describe what they saw, heard, and felt. Fortunately, this did not keep them from pouring their hearts out as they stretched to describe the indescribable. One contributor summed up the challenge this way: *"The feelings are very difficult to describe with words because they are way, way beyond that."*

Around a fourth of the experiencers stated on their questionnaire that they encountered features out of keeping with their beliefs at the time. I think it is significant that so many experiencers do not encounter what they expect. However, they seldom doubt the validity of what happened to them afterwards. Even those facing hostile disbelief from others after returning know that what they encountered is real. As one experiencer said, *"Direct experience is something no one can take from you."*

Nearly a third of the stories I received specifically speak of a love which is beyond anything known on earth. I now call the love they refer to "profound love." Many who mention this love traveled to an other-worldly place or dimension when they left their body, and I call that place or dimension "the world of love and light."

Although these stories have helped me accept the reality of life after death, I am not trying to prove life after death or any of my other conclusions. My goal is to provide enough examples to illustrate what experiencers now know about love and life beyond death. If you are interested in a more statistical approach, I recommend the book *Evidence of the Afterlife: The Science of Near-Death Experiences* by Jeffrey Long, M.D.[6]

FITTING IT ALL TOGETHER

In this book I reveal many insights experiencers have shared about love and about the world of love and light. These insights, which are most inspiring and compelling to me, have been taken from over a hundred of the accounts. As one experiencer said, *"If you put all of our stories together, you might get a good picture of a totally ineffable subject."*

In Chapter Two, we will get a taste of the love we can learn about from near-death experiences through an amazing personal account. We will also identify the sequence of events as they commonly unfold in near-death experiences.

Chapters Three through Nine each present a collection of common themes found in the stories about love. Each chapter begins with an eye-opening individual account written by one experiencer. Except for a few minor grammatical corrections, the experiencer's own words are preserved. Each introductory account is followed by a short quotation from several additional experiencers giving their perspectives regarding one of the themes in that chapter. Some quotations are found in more than one section because they are relevant to several themes.

Chapter Two

We Can Learn About Love from Near-Death Experiences

Our view of life, and how we interpret it, was so out of context and far from its origin of truth – the truth of this light that was emanating a more-than-intergalactic radiance of love. I knew that the pure state that I was in was how God had created me.

– Cecilia

Hearing about love from near-death experiencers warms my heart. I am deeply moved when they speak of the love they encountered in the world of love and light. Just listening to their stories of that pure and powerful love helps me accept that it is real and is there for all of us, including me.

Our introductory experience, from Cecilia, powerfully portrays that amazing love. It also illustrates many of the common elements of near-death experiences, which are summarized following her story. One day in 1985, at age twenty-six, Cecilia discovered a new reality, a world of love and light.

A few months after the birth of her second child, a severe staph infection almost took Cecilia's life. She had become too weak to care for her children, so her husband stayed home from work to help out. She went to lie on her bed. Suddenly she heard a loud buzzing in her ears and began to rise out of her body, floating above her house and into the treetops.

CECILIA'S EXPERIENCE

I remember thinking, "What am I doing up here?" Then coming to the conclusion, "I must be dead!" I also reflected on the fact of how silly it was that people were afraid of this. It wasn't all that bad – just floating around, pretty painless!

Rising through the sky

I continued to float and ascend simultaneously. Higher and higher – through the clouds and even higher, until I reached beyond our stratosphere, I was rising into a dark night full of beautiful, glorious stars. I felt so free, leaving the heaviness of the world behind, leaving the heaviness of me behind. I realized that I was not in physical form I had once been in. I traveled like a wisp, light as a feather.

I felt light as a feather, too. Any worries or concerns, pain, or fear, were all gone. I felt like a little child, carefree and light. I was the pure me – unscathed by the world. A true pure self. Wow, I hadn't felt that for a long time, since I was a small child. I was ecstatic!

Entering the void

But beyond the stars, as I continued to rise through their grandeur, I became aware of the fact that I was entering a new realm, a dark empty void. I saw nothing but blackness, I felt nothing but blackness. I was filled with an overwhelming fear of this black nothingness. Then I remembered something, "Yea, though I walk through the valley of the shadow of death, I will fear no evil." "I love the Lord, I will not be afraid," this is what I thought and believed with my entire existence.

At that very instant I was immediately surrounded by some sort of protective blanket of love and safety. I can only describe it as a "force field of love." I didn't know if there was anything in the darkness that could harm me, but I did know that now I was under a supernatural protection. I also began to see a tiny pinpoint of light in the distance.

Toward the light

I was drawn to the light like a moth to a flame. I passed through the dark void. I traveled closer to the light and entered a tunnel of swirling unearthly colors that seemed alive with movement. I can find no words to describe their beauty or the wonderful peace, love, and serenity I was feeling during my ascent. I had reflective deep thoughts about time and how it had no relevance there. How our view of life, and how we interpret it, was so out of context and far from its origin of truth—the truth of this light that was emanating a more-than-intergalactic radiance of love.

I knew that the pure state that I was in was how God had created me. That's why it felt so natural and "right." The person I had become was like a mixed up puzzle with a few pieces missing. And I would have never been able to find those pieces if I continued to believe that "I" was in charge of my life and being.

As I came nearer to the light, I became elated, excited, flooded with the anticipation of the great love that awaited. You know how you feel when you're going home after you've been away for a long time? You know how it feels when you turn onto that road that leads "back to it all"? That's the feeling! Utter joy and euphoria beyond words!! "Someone who really loves me is waiting!"

As I approached the light the brightness was beyond measurement in human standards. I remember thinking my eyes would probably burn out, so I attempted to reach up and shield them with my hand, but there was no earthly hand to shade any earthly eyes. I was once again elated to know that I could focus directly on the most awesome, beautiful light without fear of anything. I felt like I was drowning in God's love!

Finally—I arrived! I came to a sort of plain of mist in front of the light.

No sooner did I stop than I saw them. Three silhouettes coming toward me from the distance. They emerged from the light walking together, side by side. I knew they were coming for me, they loved me, and I them. I was so happy! I struggled to make out the figures in detail but the light was so bright it was impossible. As they came closer, two of the figures stopped, only one came forward to meet me.

Met by a robed figure

It was a robed figure, shoulder length hair, with a hood. Kindness and love vibrated through him and came into me. I was astounded and ecstatic. I loved him so much. I knew that he knew every thought I was having, and that he even knew my heart. We communicated without speaking. There was no need. I was so happy to see him, and he to see me.

He asked me if I had any regrets about being there. I answered, "No." But in that same instant a flash of my husband and my two children traveled through me, and he knew. I tried to tell him that they would be okay and that they didn't need me, but he knew better. That was when I learned I could not deceive him. He knew my every thought and feeling. He felt that instant of regret, even though I wanted him to believe I would have none. I felt ashamed that I tried to convince him otherwise.

He told me that I had not finished yet, it was not my time. I finally accepted. But I did beg to see his face. For him to come close enough for me to really see him, like an eager child. He came closer and closer. With each step my longing grew, so that I thought I would explode with elation.

He walked directly up to me and continued to walk, until he became part of me. He walked right into me. He merged with my being and filled me with complete light and complete love. It was a spiritual union of light and love.

Returning

Then I felt myself dropping down, down, so quickly . . . becoming so heavy, so heavy, then the buzzing, loud buzzing, and I opened my eyes.

I was back on my bed, back in my room.

My room was filled with such an intense light. Everything in it glowed like the special effects in a movie after a nuclear explosion. I felt so different! I got up and felt as though I walked on air. I was light as a balloon. I couldn't believe it. All my pain was gone! I could breathe, I felt like I had just been born!

I couldn't wait to see my family. I got up and walked out into the living room and there I saw my husband playing with my two children – it was as if I was seeing them for the first time. Everything was new, fresh, and good. I couldn't wait to look out the front window.

I never noticed how green a tree was before, how blue the sky, how gorgeous the world!!

As I looked out my window in awe, I heard that deep, still voice speak one more time, "We are only visitors here." I guess I needed to know that. I know I took life here for granted and at other times felt more like I was serving a sentence. Not anymore.

And I do remember the one realization I had as I ascended through the heavens was that you only take one thing with you as you pass from this existence, "LOVE."

Cecilia's beautiful account introduces many of the themes about love that are found in this book. Before we look at the major insights about love that Cecilia and others have shared, I want to review the general sequence in which events during a near-death experience often occur.

TYPICAL SEQUENCE OF EVENTS IN AN NDE

Here are the most common events that occur within a near-death experience. Not all experiencers report all of these events, as is clear from Cecilia's account. The order of events within this typical sequence may also vary greatly. For example, some people review their life immediately after leaving their body. Sometimes people find themselves directly in the light without any experience of traveling.

1. Leaving the body
2. Traveling
    a. On the earth plane
    b. Through the stars
    c. In the void
    d. Through a tunnel
3. Seeing a light
4. Arriving in the light; beautiful landscape
5. Meeting light beings, angels, Jesus, God, etc.
6. Meeting loved ones
7. Reviewing their life
8. Touring heaven
9. Wanting to stay
10. Returning to the body
11. Adjusting to after-effects

THEMES OF LOVE IN THE LIGHT

From Cecilia's first mention of a *"protective blanket of love and safety"* to her final thought that *"you only take one thing with you as you pass from this existence, LOVE,"* she shares her many discoveries about love and about the world of love and light. In this book, we will hear many wonderful things near-death experiencers have learned. The following themes are addressed in upcoming chapters:

1. *We Don't Die.* Cecilia demonstrated what some experiencers say, that there is no death. While Cecilia

doesn't state explicitly that she still had all her faculties after she left her physical body, some describe having a non-physical form, a mind, and all of their senses. Cecilia says she doesn't understand why people are afraid of death, that it *"wasn't all that bad,"* and many others say they no longer fear death after their experience. Quite a few refer to the world of love and light as their true home.

2. *The Nature of Love Is Greater Than We Ever Imagined.* Cecilia refers to *"a force field of love."* Others refer to the love as an energy, force, or vibration, and various experiencers say the love is beyond human words, unearthly, and immeasurably powerful. Some say that everything is made of love.

3. *Love Has Higher Qualities.* Cecilia mentions several qualities associated with the love she experienced. She speaks of the *"more-than-intergalactic radiance of love"* and the peace and joy she felt. Others speak of love as unconditional, non-judgmental, and all-inclusive. They say the world of love and light is a place of joy, compassion, all knowledge, and peace.

4. *Love Emanates from Many Sources.* Cecilia felt love from several sources during her near-death experience: from the force field of love, in the tunnel, from the light, *"God's love,"* from the three silhouettes,

and especially from the one who came forward. Some of the most common sources of love mentioned by experiencers are God, Jesus, the light, and a light being. Some, like Cecilia, describe multiple sources.

5. *All Are One.* Some experiencers are shown that everything is part of the one whole. Others learn that they have never been alone and never will be. Some say love is our essence and at the core of our being.

6. *There Is a Reason and Purpose for Everything.* Cecilia was told her life was not finished yet, that it was not her time, and she realized her family needed her. Regarding purpose, others say they realize that every life has a purpose, that love is the purpose of life, and that there is a reason for everything that happens, even suffering. Some report we choose our lives and have opportunities to come back for more lifetimes.

7. *In Life, Love Is Most Important.* After she returned, Cecilia remembered "*you only take one thing with you as you pass from this existence, LOVE.*" This is consistent with what other experiencers say, that love never ends. Many experiencers learn about love from their life review. They have learned the importance of choosing higher vibrations, emotions, and thoughts; of living life fully; and of treating everyone with love and kindness.

In Chapter Three, we look more closely at the question "What happens when our body dies?" A fascinating account describes one person's dying experience and her encounters with love after leaving her body. We also hear from others who help us understand that we don't die, that we still have our mind, senses, and a non-physical form, that the world of love and light is our true home, and that we don't need to fear death.

Chapter Three

We Don't Die

I remember being told that the light is produced by the love of the Divine Master, the Almighty. His love is so strong that it produces a light powerful enough to go through different realms! No matter where you are in his Kingdom, you always feel his love. – Letitia

I always believed in life after death, and had a picture in my mind of a vague, cloudy, fluffy heaven, but I had never thought about it as truly real . . . until I began listening to near-death experiences. Now that I have talked to so many people who have had near-death experiences and have read so many accounts, I understand life after death so much better. I am now convinced that heaven is real and that we are eternal beings.

First we will hear from Letitia about her experience. She discovers that death is not the end and she details some of the wonderful things she found in the next world. She describes the powerful love she encountered there and looks forward to going back some day.

LETITIA'S EXPERIENCE

Letitia was a young Canadian woman of twenty-eight, hospitalized with Guillain-Barré Syndrome.[7] She was on life-support, paralyzed from head to toe, and in excruciating pain. Then she died. Here is her story.

I used to believe that death was the end. I used to believe that life on earth was the only life we had. What happened to me altered the above statements and allowed for the most wonderful feelings to never end.

The whole experience began when I started feeling that death was coming, I can still smell it! That part, to me, is still very painful to remember. It was a slow and painful death. One day or night, I couldn't make out the difference at the end, I felt like my heart and my lungs were going to explode, I knew it was only a matter of moments.

After that critical period, the pain suddenly stopped. I opened my eyes to see if the doctors were in my room, I found it strange that the pain would suddenly stop.

I opened my eyes and saw what seemed to be a priest and a few other people. I could only see their shadows but I knew he was a religious man and I thought of the others as members of my family. I immediately assumed that the doctors had called my family and a priest (traditions, you know) for my final moments. The priest had got my attention for some reason, perhaps because he was very tall, and very attractive for a priest! There was a light coming from behind them, a very bright light. It was blinding me. I thought it was coming from the nurse's station. The priest seemed to look at me as if he was saying, "It's all right, you can go." I closed my eyes and I let myself go.

In a matter of seconds, I started viewing periods of my life, everything flashing before me as if it was on a reel of film scrolling upwards really fast. After the viewing, I felt ready to go. I then felt some kind of pressure coming from inside my body and out through my mouth. I knew that was my last breath. Everything went silent.

A few moments after that, I felt I was still around. I opened my eyes again to see what was going on and I saw the priest still standing at the foot of my bed with the others. He started communicating with me without talking. He explained what was happening to me. I understood what he was telling me the second he was thinking it. My questions were answered as I was thinking them. I don't remember if I have communicated with the other beings, but I know they were there as some kind of followers, or students.

I just couldn't believe that only the body dies. I was still able to think, to look, to feel!!

Escort to the light

I *wanted to know more (I have an adventurous mind). He told me I will know more and that he had been sent to escort me to the light. I was able to see that light coming from behind them, the same light which I thought was coming from the nurse's station.*

He then told me it was time to go. I guess he felt I was insecure; he took my hand and looked at me with such tenderness (if I would have had my heart still, it would have melted for sure). I will never forget his beautiful and deep eyes. I felt his love and compassion, his confidence and his knowledge all at once. His love was filling me with warmth! I wasn't worried anymore. I trusted him; I even had the impression that I knew him and he knew me.

In the tunnel

I then felt some kind of vibrations, and I felt I was being sucked up in a whirling motion, at an incredible speed, into a large dark tunnel. In a matter of maybe (earth time) a few seconds, I found myself on my back, the palm of my hands up and my feet pointing forward. It seemed to be a symbolic position. I remember looking at myself and realizing that I was no longer attached to my body. In my mind, the memory of my body was still fresh so I had the impression to still be in it even though I wasn't. I guess it would be like looking in a mirror and not seeing your reflection.

As we were going through the tunnel, I heard beautiful music, very soft singing, or more like humming. I felt elevated by the music. I felt peace and comfort.

In the light

As we reached the light, the feelings became very intense. It was the most beautiful thing I had ever felt! I thought it was such a cool and fascinating experience. I must have asked what it was that I was feeling so strongly coming from the light, because I remember being told that the light is produced by the love of the Divine Master, the Almighty. His love is so strong that it produces a light powerful enough to go through different realms! No matter where you are in his Kingdom, you always feel his love.

I felt as if I was embraced by the light. I became one with it. I felt free, I felt very much alive, I felt complete. The feelings are very difficult to describe with words because they are way, way beyond that.

Re-entering the physical body

I wish that moment would have lasted for eternity, but for reasons still unknown to me today, I had to come back. As I was in the comfort of the light, I suddenly felt myself being sucked down in the same fashion I had gone up. The motion abruptly stopped, and my soul slowly reentered my body. I then felt very cold, very very cold, and I was feeling aches and pains all over again.

I opened my eyes and my suspicions were confirmed, I was back in my body, in the hospital room. I didn't understand why I was back, I wanted to stay in that beautiful place, I wanted to learn more about it, I wanted to explore. I wanted to stay with my dear angel. I was missing him already. I felt like a part of me was missing. I was thinking about what had just happened and I felt his hand gently touching my head. I felt comforted and secure and fell asleep.

Recovery

From that moment on, my health quickly improved. The doctors were amazed at my recovery.

I have talked to my family about what had happened to me but no one seemed to really want to discuss it. It is only years later that I have learned that in fact, at one time they thought I was dead, but I came back. Well it isn't just a thought to me; I have died and come back.

I will always feel blessed by the experience and I'll forever be grateful for what I have seen, felt, and most importantly, learned. I know I will go back when the time is right. I have to. Like the song "I left my heart in San Francisco," well I left mine in Heaven!

Letitia's story uplifts my heart every time I read it. I am grateful to her for sharing her discoveries about life after death. It was clear to Letitia that she was still around and many other experiencers also mention that not only were they still alive but they still had their mind and senses. Some describe how they looked outside their physical body. Many say the world of love and light they visited is their true home. While Letitia anticipates returning to the world of love and light some day, quite a few explicitly state they no longer fear death.

ONLY OUR BODY DIES

Like Letitia, many others also say they now know that life continues after death. Here are some of the ways others describe what they learned about the continuity of life after death from their experiences.

Cassandra was forty-seven when she was innertubing down a river in Texas, went over a waterfall, and drowned. *"There is absolutely nothing to fear about death, that isn't even a good word for it. It's like going through a doorway. One minute you are on the inside, and the next you step into the outside. No loss of consciousness, no pain, just pure bliss on the other side."*

Joanna had a reaction to anesthesia prior to surgery and went to a warm, comfortable, dark place. Later, reflecting on her experience, she said, *"It was not a dream. It was very, very real. I also have no doubt in my mind that our energy and minds go on after death."*

Dino died from an allergic reaction and now knows we are not our bodies. He explains, *"I was in the emergency room and*

I could hear them saying, 'He's gone. We lost him.' And yet I could see and hear, but not with my eyes or ears. I just knew. I moved toward the light (bright). I knew who I am is not my body, I am my awareness. I don't stop being. I felt better than I have ever felt, more loved. I was home. This isn't home, that is . . . I know we are not our bodies and that everyone has a wonderful surprise coming, at what they call the end. It is a beginning, a change of form is all. Direct experience is something no one can take from you. Only you can do that by forgetting the gift it offers you. I tell you and anyone who listens, we are more than this body." Dino reports that since his experience, *"My health is perfect. I don't get sick. I can't. I know who I am."* He also reports that he now sees auras and he seems to know things without anything being said. He now trusts *"this process we call life,"* and is studying philosophy and spiritual ideas.

Dawn was delivering twins by C-section when she left her body and traveled through the roof of the hospital and above the town. She chose to return because she remembered her children. She learned that only the body gives out. She reports, *"Before the experience, I believed that when you die, you're dead. You just go out like the last flicker of a flame. No thoughts, no memories, no nothing. My oldest daughter was murdered when she was 16 years old. I know that having had an NDE is what got me through her passing because I know she is okay. I thank God every day for allowing me to know that only the body gives out, the 'me' goes on and on."*

Joan was experiencing extreme grief following the death of her husband. One day she fell asleep and left her body, moved through a vortex, and came to a place where she was greeted. *"There were no words, just an understanding. I was jubilant, calm, loved, loving. I understood that death is an illusion and that there is a veil, a curtain, ever so thin, between what we know as 'life' and what we know as 'death.'"*

WE HAVE OUR MIND, SENSES, AND A NON-PHYSICAL FORM

Letitia states she was still able to think, look and feel, and upon entering the tunnel, she felt like she was still in a body. Here are selections from other experiencers who mention having some type of non-material body after they leave their physical one, and who clearly still have command of their mind and senses.

Berenice was twenty-two when she slipped in the bathroom and was knocked out by hitting her chin on the sink. When she first went out of her physical body, she felt as though she looked like this: *"I seemed to be 'a ball of consciousness,' no real shape."* However, later, after going upward at high speed and coming to a stop in front of four beings, she perceived herself differently. She noticed how her arm looked. *"I felt as though I looked like I look now, only I was made out of light. I wore a long flowing white dress. I reached out my hand to the beings, and I looked down at my arm. It looked just like my arm looks now, except it was made out of illuminating light. The beings took hold of my hand."*

Stella, a self-proclaimed atheist, was eighteen when she stopped breathing while taking drugs. After moving in and out of consciousness for a while, she decided that she was ready to go. Here she describes what happened as she moved toward the light and entered it. *"At that moment, I started traveling at an incredible speed – indescribably fast – and I also became aware of two beings next to me traveling with me. The faster we went, the lighter I became and the more energy I gained – I was bursting with joy and happiness – all sense of anything painful, heavy, fearful, anxious – it was absolutely nonexistent to me. I was this ball of joyous happiness.*

"When I arrived finally, I was overwhelmed with happiness and momentarily lost as I tried to make sense of what I was sensing and feeling and seeing – it was the most beautiful landscape, undescribable by human terms because we don't have such beauty here – there was a soft light permeating everything and I saw around five to eight light beings rush towards me – they weren't pure white, rather had some coloring inside them – bluish/violet. And I looked down on my own left hand to see that I was made of the same thing as them – this bubbling light-filled energy blob."

Kathie was nineteen, riding in the back seat of a car with friends, when her heart began to race and she felt nauseous. She left her body, saw it from above the car, and began moving through space with stars and planets passing by very quickly. She entered a white room or space and interacted with beings there for some time before encountering a barrier in the form of a line. This is when she first noticed her appearance. *"I then looked down and saw a line. My foot (Yes, I did have a 'spiritual body' as did the others I encountered) was stepping over the line to go to be with the others. Then I was told 'If you cross that line, you can't go back. It would mean you would have to die.' Funny as it may sound, up to that point I didn't realize that I would have to die or was about to die. It never occurred to me. I didn't realize that I was separate from my body even though I had seen it in the car. I felt complete. I remember thinking this isn't how I pictured death."* Other experiencers also report coming to a boundary. They understand that their death will be final if they cross it. A boundary can take various forms, for example, a river or a fence.

Dawn, who left her body during the C-section, describes herself two ways. When she first went out of her body, she rose up and gently hit the ceiling. At that point she says, *"I felt like an electrically charged ball of cotton."* Later, after moving upward through the ceiling and beyond the hospital, she noticed, *"I had a body. When I looked down, I saw my feet and was surprised because I had not been able to just glance down and see my feet for several months, as the last time I looked I was eight months pregnant with twins. I glanced backward and saw a long silver cord*[8] *trailing behind me that I assumed was some kind of tie attached to the gown I was wearing. I can only describe this gown as a material made from crushed opals, diamonds and butterfly wings. My thought was, 'I'm going to have to cut this sash when I get where I'm going or I'll be tripping over it.'"*

When Montague was eighteen, he was in a British hospital with pleurisy. His brief out-of-body experience includes his perception of a (silver?) cord and also shows that his will was still intact. One night he woke up and *"felt as if there was a great weight on my chest and I was in considerable pain. Then the pain lifted and I felt myself floating above the bed. I was able to look down at my body and there seemed to be some sort of a line connecting 'me' to my body. I was being drawn away and it was a pleasant sensation. I was aware that I was being taken from my body but I did not want to go. I struggled against the pull and gradually seemed to pull myself back down."*

Davey died of starvation as a Japanese prisoner of war during World War II. He left his body and was ecstatic to discover that he felt no pain. While he didn't mention his appearance there, he observed that he had senses and a mind. Davey relates, *"I did not want to go back to my aching body. I felt complete without it. I could see, hear, think, move."*

THE WORLD OF LOVE AND LIGHT IS OUR TRUE HOME

While Letitia doesn't mention it, one of the most common claims of experiencers is that they feel they have come home when they arrive on the other side.

Lynn drowned when she was five. She says, *"When I reached the point of light I found myself in a world of light . . . Suddenly I remembered this place. This was my home, the place that was really my home, and I wondered how I could've ever forgotten about it."*

Elliott was twenty-six when he died from a drug overdose. Following an extensive visit in the white light, he says, *"It was the most exhilarating and loving feeling I ever had experienced. I had finally come home I thought."* Following this experience, he quit taking and selling drugs, and became obsessed with learning what happened to him because *"the experience was very different from the typical hallucinatory effects"* he was familiar with.

Agnes was a passenger in a car during an accident. She describes how she felt after visiting the light: *"I never ever wanted to leave it – I had come 'home.'"*

Kit was twenty-four when she bled to death after an emergency C-section. She left her body and traveled toward a distant light. She says, *"It felt like going home after being gone a long time."*

Davin was five when his heart stopped during corrective oral surgery. After finding himself in a horrid place of darkness and utter emptiness, he was drawn toward a source of comfort and heat that he knew was light. He says, *"This place felt like my natural home, like I belonged. I was enveloped by the warmth, and found myself alone with the being of warmth. I NEVER (to this day) have felt the acceptance, love, peace and sensation of full existence I felt that day."*

Stella, the atheist who overdosed at eighteen, shares, *"I KNEW this was home and I was finally who I really am – I was this absolutely beautiful being of love and innocence and I had sooo much joy and happiness."*

Didier drowned during an accident at sea while working on a research vessel as deep-sea diver and chief engineer. He says, *"I went into the light. There, in the light, I was met by others and it felt like coming home. I experienced a loving and acceptance like I had never felt before."*

Devin was thirty-one when the car in which he was riding was hit by a truck. He headed toward the light. He declares, *"I felt completely a part of this place and very much at home. I did not want to leave this place."*

Berenice, who slipped in the bathroom and was knocked out, went to a place of love, peace and comfort where she met a being of light. She says, *"The being of light . . . hugged me and said 'Ahh.' Like you would hold a new baby. I felt that I was at home with the being of light."*

Alice hemorrhaged after the birth of her third child. She says, *"I started floating upward in total darkness. I remember feeling this incredible sense of peace as I was floating upward. I felt like I was going home. I was very happy and I was not experiencing the pain in my abdomen like I had been feeling just moments before . . . I now know that death is not something to be feared. It is glorious! I truly felt as if I was going home. Peace, love, tranquility, and no pain! Wow! It was great!"*

WE DON'T NEED TO FEAR DEATH

Letitia said she left her heart in heaven and knows she will go back when the time is right. Many experiencers say they no longer have any fear of death.

Agatha remembers extreme pain and going in and out of her body as she was being born. She met "a figure" who was full of light and who knew, loved and accepted her. She reports, *"I was also left with the awareness that one day I would go home and the figure would meet me. I know the figure is always with me, and I have no fear of death because I am not alone."*

Dee was fourteen when she died of Rocky Mountain spotted fever. She says, *"I didn't and still don't fear death; there is a much better place awaiting."*

Tim, who died from an allergic reaction, reports: "*When my time finally does come again, I will welcome it. I've learned there is no need to be afraid of what will happen to us after we die.*"

Devin, who died when a truck hit the car in which he was riding, says, "*I do not fear death at all now, life has taken on a different perspective.*"

Marsha was twenty-three when she left her body due to an IV dye reaction. She went into the light. She later stated, "*I am not afraid and am so looking forward to the beauty, peace, and love that I had then.*"

Lee was praying silently while awaiting a dental procedure when she left her body. She says, "*Because I sense that what I experienced is actually how a person 'transitions' from this lifetime to their 'journey' (or death, as we call it), I have lost my fear of the dying experience and actually will greet it with open arms when it finally occurs. Not that I want to die until my time is 'due'—it's just that there was a knowledge imparted to me during the experience that we will be in a totally loving environment when we leave this earth.*"

Letitia and others showed us that we don't die—only the physical body dies. She and others say they still have their mind and senses as well as a non-physical form. They report that when they left their physical body, they went to their true home. Most experiencers no longer fear death.

Chapter 4 seeks to answer the question, "What is love?" Our introductory account will illustrate some major ways in which profound love differs from earthly love. We go on to examine the true nature of love, as reported by experiencers.

Chapter Four

The Nature of Love Is Greater Than We Ever Imagined

I was enveloped in a LOVE I could not put into words. This DIVINE LOVE was in everything and in me. At the core of my being, I was this LOVE and so was everyone else.

– Helen

I have heard incredible things that I could never have imagined about the nature of love from near-death experiences. Near-death and other mystical experiencers talk about love as an energy or power, and this I think I can grasp. But they also say things like "everything is made out of love," which continues to stretch my understanding. However, since I believe that God created everything and that God is love, I have come to accept that God made all creation out of that love. This includes me, you, and all humanity.

Our introductory account was written by Helen, a woman who had an inexplicable experience in her forties that changed her life. A greater reality was revealed to her through meditation. Although Helen doesn't speak of traveling to another world, she comes out of a deep meditation with an awareness of the same profound love many near-death experiencers report. In this chapter, we will look at what she and others say about the nature of that love.

HELEN'S EXPERIENCE

I had been meditating every afternoon for the last year and a half. On this lovely spring day, upon completing my meditation, I arose with the calmness and peace associated with a lengthy meditative state. I went downstairs to my living room and I noticed as I looked out the window that I was ONE with the blades of grass and the rocks in the road. I was enveloped in a LOVE I could not put into words. This DIVINE LOVE was in everything and in me. At the core of my being, I was this LOVE and so was everyone else.

Remaining in a state of grace

In this state, which I refer to as a state of Grace, there was no right or wrong, no good or bad, no judgment whatsoever. Fear was non-existent! There was no death and I knew that we all live forever. Everyone I met was LOVE. It did not matter what they looked like, behaved like. I was they and they were me. We are all connected. The utter joy is indescribable. I knew we did not end at our fingertips. The peace and bliss are beyond words.

I became aware that a Presence other than what I usually think of as myself was looking through my eyes. I had become ONE with this INFINITE AWARENESS that simply sees without judgment. It is the very essence of life, eternal life. I wanted nothing, needed nothing. It was PEACE that passeth understanding.

My family and friends kept asking me about this deep calmness they observed in me. I could not translate this verbally to them at the time. It just flowed through me and out to all. I began to realize that in response to questions asked, the answers came from some deep place of wisdom within that knew Truth.

Winning and losing do not matter

I was at a ballgame in North Carolina and my son was pitching for his college team. It was a particularly important championship game for him and normally I would have been wringing my hands with every pitch and jumping up and down with each strikeout. This day I found myself sitting and watching the game in a state of Bliss, just indescribable. My son's girlfriend came up to me and asked if I was all right. I said, "Why of course, I'm fine." She said, "You seem so calm and Mike has the bases loaded and you're not nervous." The reply from my lips was, "Honey, winning and losing do not matter." Upon seeing her reaction, I fully realized she did not understand. How could she? I realized I needed to just live it and not try to explain what I was experiencing. How could I explain that nothing was needed, for all was given.

A drunk is worthy and loved

Also, during this period of time, I recall seeing a man who was drunk and disheveled sitting on a curb. As I approached him, I saw his True Being. He was LOVE. There was no judgment. He was as worthy as everyone else. He was loved as much as everyone else. I understood I was seeing beyond appearances.

This is our natural state

I also understood that this is our natural state. This is how we are meant to live. It did not matter what I did or had. There was Joy in every act, every chore, every occasion. LOVE and JOY pervaded everything. The energy of the universe is LOVE and it flows through us all. We are all a part of this LOVE. We are all ONE with GOD.

Return to ordinary reality

For two glorious weeks, I went to sleep with a smile on my face and awoke smiling in utter joy. On the fourteenth day, I was having a telephone conversation with my mother and she too had noticed a change in my voice and attitude. She always would ask me what caused such a profound change and I guess on this day I felt I 'should' tell her, and when I did attempt it, I believe I tried to personalize it and it dissipated as suddenly as it had appeared.

I couldn't believe it! I didn't know what to do. I was now in ordinary reality, or the relative world as I've come to call it, but with the Knowledge of the Greater Truth/GOD. "How do I live like this?" I asked.

It was most difficult to listen to the world news, to see how we are to each other. This realization has changed me forever. I could not, would not, turn my back on this. I became involved in helping the homeless and the hungry. I have Love in my heart for everyone, regardless of what they look like, behave like.

It is so necessary for me to speak with others who have touched this LOVE. This experience came upon me in the spring of 1985, but it is as if it happened just yesterday, for every detail is as clear now as then.

Earth's spiritual evolution

It is my belief that we are in the infancy stage of our spiritual evolution and all the millions of near-death experiencers and those of us who have had mystical experiences are contributing to the next stage of our development. It is my hope that as more and more of us grow in Truth and number, we will one day, indeed, have Heaven on Earth. Then we will be living as all the Masters have taught, loving our neighbors as ourselves.

How my life changed

My life changed as a result of my experience in the following ways. I became more tolerant of others. I feel more compassion for my fellow human beings, even those that commit what we consider in our relative world to be unforgivable crimes. I've become less reactive, not as quick to get angry. I have also become much less fearful.

For several years after my experience, tremendous travail came upon several family members, and without the strength and clarity and faith accorded me in 1985, I doubt I would have been able to sustain such tragedy so well. I guess what I am trying to say is that you know who you really are on a deep level. You identify more with spirit than with your ego. You feel more loving toward yourself and certainly very accepting of yourself and hence others. You realize you need not punish yourself in any way as a result of the limiting belief in retribution so many of us have been taught.

In addition, it became natural to give over to God and let go. Also, much more of an ability to surrender in all ways with non-judgment, lightness, joy and love. People that pushed my buttons before no longer had any influence in that respect. I saw that their need to create dissension came from their fear and lack of self-love, which in turn released compassion and forgiveness within me and toward them, which was healing for all.

The sacredness of all life

Before I close I have to add that perhaps the most important aspect for me has been the knowledge of the sacredness of all life. To know that we are all connected in spirit and to have witnessed the ONENESS of all creation in a state of LOVE and BLISS is to glimpse GOD. The experience of feeling something other than myself as myself, yet that had its own identity, has changed my perspective on life and death in a way that is difficult to express.

Helen's incredible account offers valuable information about the nature of the love she brought back from her meditation. We will look at some of her statements and those of others concerning several aspects of the nature of profound love.

LOVE IS BEYOND HUMAN WORDS

Helen used the terms "indescribable," "beyond words," and "passeth understanding" in portraying the peace, bliss, and joy she felt after her meditation. Many near-death experiencers report that there is no adequate way to put into words, or describe in earthly terms, the profound love they experienced on the other side. Here is what they say about this impossibility:

Deborah was seven when she had foot surgery. She met angels at the entrance to a tunnel. Although the angels would not allow her to enter the tunnel, she reports, "*I was filled with deep peace, love, happiness and warmth . . . It was the most extraordinary and beautiful experience I ever had or have ever had. The peace and warmth and happiness I felt are beyond human words."*

Letty's heart stopped during an eclamptic convulsion the day after she gave birth, and she headed toward the light. She states, "*The closer I came to that light, the more overwhelmed I was by beauty, love, and peace. I have an English degree and I am a writer, but I do not have words to describe the unconditional love and acceptance I felt."*

Adrian was undergoing heart bypass surgery when he found himself in a beautiful landscape where he sensed the presence of other beings. He states, "*The feelings I experienced of overwhelming love, peace, and joy cannot be expressed in words."*

Jake was in a hospital recovering from a serious illness when he shot out of his body and was held by an unidentified being. Of his experience, he said: "*I felt this sense of being loved that I have not felt before or since. It was a kind of love that I really can not describe."*

Davey, who died of starvation as a prisoner of war, attempts to describe how he felt during his near-death experience. "*A great inrush of love and ecstasy filled my being. It seemed as if I was on the very point of dissolving, like a thin wire with too much electrical energy flowing through it. Words cannot adequately convey the rapture; it was almost too much joy for one man's lifetime."*

Morie had a heart attack, left his body, and found himself floating over a lake churning with beautiful colors. He says, *"I had this overwhelming feeling of absolute love, peace, or whatever the word you want to use to describe this feeling. Nothing I can say can possibly come even close!"*

A former skeptic, Morie also offers an interesting confession, now that he understands that near-death experiences are real: *"I always took these stories of people seeing the proverbial 'light at the end of the tunnel' with tongue in cheek. I couldn't help but think that most of these people had heard of this story and, in order to stand in their own 'fifteen minutes of fame,' made this up when they found out that they had come close to death. Well, I now stand corrected, and I apologize to all of those whom I thought this of. Now that I have been there, I not only totally believe their stories, but I understand their inability to describe it! For, the fact is, it is impossible to describe it properly!"*

Veronika suffered a serious head injury in an automobile accident. She says, *"I was in an area that I will describe in human terms, but, well . . . I was aware of white robe, feet, sandals, whiteness like brilliant clouds beneath me/us, above, around, all over, but the awareness of the presence and His 'words' about not being my time, and go back and give of M/myself (both of us as He is in me), were not heard with ears or seen with eyes, but clearer (?!), and I see them with my mind's eyes and ears now."* Regarding her experience, she could barely contain the exuberance she felt: *"Oh, to touch my Lord's presence, realize the Love and peace, to touch just a glimpse of eternity, wonderful, joy, ohhh, human words do not describe it."*

When Rosalie was twenty, she felt that no one cared for her or loved her. Her experience occurred after she tried to kill herself and was revived. At first she didn't remember what had happened, but when she was told, her first thought was, *"Oh no. Now what is my boyfriend going to think of me?"* Immediately, the room lit up and *"pure love filled the whole room and filled me, too."* A voice spoke to her and said, *"WHO CARES WHAT HE THINKS! I HAVE GIVEN YOUR LIFE BACK TO YOU. THIS IS MY GIFT TO YOU. GO FORWARD, AND LIVE YOUR LIFE TO ITS FULLEST."* Next she says, *"I then had the pleasure of bathing in the most incredible, most loving sense of—well, I don't know how to describe it—just pure love and pure understanding. I simply was loved and adored. I felt very understood. I can't get over that feeling I had that day. It was by far the most incredible experience I have ever been through. Sends chills down my spine when I think back to it. Wow."*

Moira was raped and choked to death. She left her body and found herself standing by the bed. She ran and tried to call the police, but couldn't pick up the phone. Then she realized she was dead and began floating upward. At first she feared she was going to hell because she felt such hatred for the person raping her. However, she says, "*Then I was in a comforting, golden light . . . I was surrounded with love beyond belief.*"

PROFOUND LOVE IS UNEARTHLY

When Helen speaks of "Divine Love," her use of the term "divine" implies that the love she felt was not from earth. Several experiencers specifically acknowledge the unearthly nature of the profound love they encountered on the other side.

Derval left her body during an episode of extreme emotional anguish. She describes the love she felt: "*Before I knew it, I was floating up, UP. Then I saw the most beautiful mountains I had ever seen and the sky was breathtaking. An indescribable feeling of ultimate love swept over me. All I can say is that it did not feel like an earthly love at all. It was very different and very warming, comforting, and wonderful. I was truly happy, just floating there; I could have stayed there forever.*"

Blake died during a surgical procedure in a Dutch hospital. He went out of his body, through a short tunnel, and into a bright space where he knew everything about everybody who was there. He says, "*The most important feeling was the waves of love, nothing to fear, love as we don't know here on earth.*"

Patrick was sixteen in 1967 when he was in a serious multi-car accident on a rainy day. Unlike earthly love, the love Patrick felt during his near-death experience was physically palpable. "*I could see the beautiful light ahead of me and the warm wonderful love that was radiating from that source. I was moving toward that light and feeling more and more at home in that new world. But, before I could embrace God, I was told that it was not my time and that I had to go back. I was very sorrowful that I could not stay. I did not want to be separated from that love that was so physically palpable."*

Sidonia left her body during a minor outpatient surgical procedure. She went into space, through a tunnel, and then into another world where she met Jesus. She says, *"OH, what a feeling of Love and true joy that has never been felt before . . . NOTHING, NOTHING on earth could compare to what I was feeling."*

LOVE IS ENERGY, VIBRATION, FORCE

Helen stated that she experienced love as the energy of the universe. Others also speak of love as energy, and some use the words "vibration" or "force" to describe the profound love.

Sorcha, from Ireland, was killed in an automobile accident while traveling in New Zealand. In an instant she was *"somewhere else, full of Love, Light and friends."* She describes the love. *"The place I was in was so full of Love, Love as an ENERGY rather than an Emotion. Unconditional Love is an energy . . . in being all that there is, was or ever will be. LOVE IS THE ENERGY OF CREATION."*

Judd had a heart attack at age fifty-one. Time seemed to stop, and he found himself viewing a grid of stars against a black background, when he heard a voice. Love is one of the words Judd uses to describe the energy that envelops him at that moment. *"Words such as Love, serenity, peace, joy, lightness come to mind to describe the energy which completely envelopes and fills my being . . . Somehow I feel that the Energy which enveloped me has remained with me."*

Joan, who was experiencing extreme grief following the death of her husband and left her body, says, *"I was vibrating at an extraordinary rate – what I can only describe as being like a current of electricity."* She moved through a vortex, and came to a place where she was greeted by someone. Later she referred to the love she felt there: *"I've experienced real love and I know what it means and so much of what surrounds me is at odds with it . . . My own sense is that love – the kind of sensation I experienced, whether we call it love or something else – is a particular vibration and maybe that is the vibrational sense I experienced."*

Jessica was twenty-six when she died during childbirth. After an ecstatic journey into the light, she was unexpectedly "zapped back" into her body and quickly gave birth to a healthy baby girl. Years later, after the death of her sister, she reflected on her own dying experience. She speaks of love as a "force." *"The most important realization I came to is that the force of the universe is love."*

Cecilia, who died of the staph infection following childbirth, found herself in a dark place that terrified her, and she repeated a line from the twenty-third Psalm, "*Yea, though I walk through the valley of the shadow of death, I will fear no evil.*" She describes the love she felt then as a "force field." "*At that very instant I was immediately surrounded by some sort of protective blanket of love and safety. I can only describe it as a 'force field of love.'*"

LOVE IS IMMEASURABLY POWERFUL

Although Helen doesn't explicitly describe the power of the love she experienced, she writes "LOVE" in all caps, implying that it is more than ordinary love. Others, however, refer specifically to the immeasurably powerful nature of the love they encounter, often by contrasting it with human love.

Veronika, who received the serious head injury in an automobile accident, describes the intensity of the love she felt during her near-death experience this way: "*I have told someone recently, imagine the feeling of love with someone you love more than anyone or anything else you have ever loved. Now magnify that feeling by billions and trillions and more and more gigabytes that are on every computer in the world and then you may come close to what I felt.*"

Gillian was in an induced coma prior to surgery for a bleeding brain aneurysm when she "*woke up*" and saw "*little white lights floating all around"* her. She recounted, *"There was a shadow of a man in a coat and hat to the left side of my head. I couldn't see His face, just His shadow, but His presence comforted me. The feeling I experienced is totally unexplainable – nothing on this earth can even compare to it. It was like God had wrapped His arms around me and filled me with His love. You know how much you love your family? Well, this feeling of love was immeasurable – 100,000 times that! It was so awesome! I wanted to go with God right then and there."*

Melisse had a high fever from German measles when she was seven years old. She closed her eyes and *"felt a very peaceful, calm sensation."* She was approached by what she could only call a cloud, and she heard what sounded like millions of voices harmonizing. Here's how Melisse described the degree of love she felt at that moment: *"I felt like I was wrapped in a warm security blanket, very cozy and safe. The love that I felt was inexpressible. Imagine all the love you've ever felt from someone (or everyone) in your life multiplied by about a million. That's how much love I felt."*

Rocky was driving with friends, shortly after graduating from high school, on a remote Alaskan road when he dozed off, ran off the road, awoke, and overcorrected causing the car to roll. He found himself in total darkness and reports, *"The only human emotion I could feel was pure, unrelenting, unconditional love. Take the unconditional love a mother has for a child and amplify it a thousand fold, then multiply exponentially. The result of your equation would be as a grain of sand is to all the beaches in the world. So, too, is the comparison between the love we experience on earth to what I felt during my experience. This love is so strong, that words like 'love' make the description seem obscene. It was the most powerful and compelling feeling. But, it was so much more."*

Stella, the eighteen-year-old atheist who overdosed on drugs, attempts to describe the love she felt when she arrived in the light. *"Right then, the most beautifully loving, unconditionally accepting force enveloped me—I was melting in the love—it's undescribable—if you were to picture the love a parent has for their child and magnified that by infinity, it still wouldn't be able to convey the love I felt."*

Sorcha, who died in the car accident in New Zealand, had this to say about the power of the love: *"I felt amazing Peace and Love so powerful that there are no words to describe the enormity, eternal energy of love and pure acceptance."*

EVERYTHING IS MADE OF LOVE

Helen told of her experience that love was in everything and was at the core of each one of us. A few other experiencers try to express the nature of the profound love as the substance of which everything is made.

Walt was being treated for depression by breathing a high-oxygen mixture when he went out of his body, had a life review, and went down a tunnel, through darkness, past a bright force, and into a bright room. Walt speaks of what he learned at that moment about love. *"It was then that it became obvious to me, either through revelation or intuition, that REALITY IS LOVE. Love has dimension, it has substance; it is not only a verb, it is a noun. To me this was the greatest gift of the whole experience knowing that Love and our souls are one."*

Agnes was in an automobile accident at age fifty-one when she found herself going down a tunnel, picking up speed, heading toward the light. Here is what Agnes says about the love: *"Then I simply gave myself up to the all-enveloping love that was surrounding me. A love that can never be described in words. It is the love of the universe. It is the universe. It is the source of all being."*

In this chapter, we have heard from Helen and other experiencers who have tried to describe the love they encountered on the other side. They told us that words don't do it justice, that it is unearthly, that it could be considered an energy, vibration or force, that it is immeasurably powerful, and that it is the substance behind all reality. Clearly, this love's nature is beyond our full knowing here on earth.

In the next chapter, we will look for answers to the question, "What are love's characteristics?" Our fascinating introductory account identifies some of the qualities experiencers most commonly mention when describing love and the world of love and light.

Chapter Five

Love Has Higher Qualities

> *The warmth and unconditional love was the first part of my experience. Being given the understanding that we are not going to be 'judged before we can enter heaven.'* – *Tim*

I first heard of unconditional love from Elisabeth Kübler-Ross and Mother Theresa. At first, I couldn't believe love could or even should be unconditional. However, after hearing about love from near-death experiences, I have begun to grasp what unconditional love can be like. The qualities and characteristics of love reported in near-death experiences require me to stretch every day.

In our introductory account, Tim has a sudden allergic reaction to medication and falls to the bathroom floor. He was only twenty-nine, in 1992, when he encountered a love that was unconditional and non-judgmental. Others describe the love as all-inclusive, as well. In addition to these qualities, many also tell about the peace, compassion, joy, and limitless knowledge they found in the world of love and light.

TIM'S EXPERIENCE

It all started after an allergic reaction to a basic anti-inflammatory. The initial reaction happened very suddenly that morning. As I lay on the bathroom floor I was drifting in and out of consciousness as my wife was on the phone getting help. The last conscious memory I had before my NDE was of a fireman escorting my wife out of the room as the paramedics started working on me.

Into the light

Suddenly I felt from above and behind me an incredibly warm, bright light appear. I was immediately drawn to it. I recalled thinking to myself that "this is amazing, I've got to check this out." With that thought I was instantly flying towards and into the light. Once I was there I was met by someone. I do not know who it was, but I know I was welcome.

While I was there I experienced many wonderful things. Things from warmth and unconditional love to having access to limitless knowledge, to the falling away of endless 'physical' boundaries. This I later called 'expanded consciousness.' I will never forget these events as I can still 'feel' them. The warmth and unconditional love was the first part of my experience. [I was] given the understanding that we are not going to be 'judged before we can enter Heaven,' that we are on this plain of existence in order to experience what it is like to physically feel.

Our true state of existence is one of pure energy, one where time has no meaning or relevance. We have no limits, boundaries and few rules. It is a state of pure energy, bliss and love.

Limitless knowledge

Next was the experience of 'limitless knowledge.' Although I was not able to retain and bring back all the knowledge that I had access to, I remember what I experienced and that I was allowed to 'see' . . . Any questions that I could think of were instantly answered.

After this I recall seeing my true self . . . The feeling of seeing myself in my true state is almost indescribable.

I have to return

As the experience continued, I was met again by the same 'spirit' or 'entity' that met me upon arrival. I was told that I was to return, for now. That it was not time for me to be back home yet, that I still had things to do. I did not want to leave but knew that I must.

The return was instant, with the flash of a light and jolting, not as warm and pleasing as the ascent. As I opened my eyes, I saw the paramedic kneeling over me with a paddle in each hand ready to 'zap' me . . . I think he was more surprised than I. This entire experience lasted, in reality, only 30 seconds. But while I was there, time was irrelevant.

Tim mentions numerous qualities of the world of love and light. Let's look at some of the most common qualities that Tim and others describe.

LOVE IS UNCONDITIONAL

Tim refers to the love he felt when he was in the light as unconditional. Others speak of unconditional love as well.

Lee was sitting in a dentist's waiting room, praying to relax herself, when she felt herself being pulled out of her body through the top of her head. She recalls the unconditional love she felt during her near-death-like experience. *"I felt and saw an extremely bright light that held loving feelings at every point. I felt intense unconditional LOVE, totally! I had never felt anything like this before and I wanted to continue this journey to see where it would take me."*

Marsha, who had an acute reaction to IV dye, spoke of an unusual entrance into the light where she found unconditional love. *"I disappeared into the stoma of a leaf and came out into a brilliant light, comparable to nothing on this earth, not even the sun, not even close."* There she found *"lots of love and a definite sense of being loved unconditionally."*

Tabitha was experiencing a financial and spiritual crisis when she had a near-death-like dream in which she was in the presence of Mother Mary and experienced unconditional love from her. She reports, *"Then all of a sudden she was with me. I was wrapped in a love so deep and so unconditional! It was actually a physical sensation like being wrapped in a blanket. Except it permeated every cell in my body and surrounded me and sustained me. Then she showed me my life. In a matter of seconds we saw every single thing I'd ever done from the time I was born. The good things, the bad things and some terrible things. All the while, I could feel the love radiating off her and from her like a radio wave directed at me. As we looked at my life, I kept expecting to feel the love change, especially when we saw the things I was ashamed of, but it never wavered an instant. Not a speck. It was strong and unconditional and pure. A human mind could never imagine a love like that."*

Kit, who was twenty-four when she bled to death after an emergency C-section, reported this about unconditional love: *"The light 'told' me I had never been alone, that I had always been loved and will always be loved no matter what, because God is unconditional love. (At age 12 my mother had told me she wished I was never born; I had begun to self-destruct instead of forgiving her.) God let me know I was okay no matter what."*

Miles had a brain aneurysm that ruptured at age twenty-three, causing him to wreck his car. He says, *"I was shown that*

God, in whatever form He is worshiped, EXISTS and cares for each and every one of us, without condition."

Lydia was a newly recovering alcoholic at age thirty-three, going through a painful divorce and facing financial ruin, when she was in a serious car crash. She speaks of the unconditional love: *"The 'real me' – my spirit – left my body and united in a blissfully personal Love sharing with God. In this Union I experienced several 'things' simultaneously: – I knew/understood that I had never done anything in my life to merit being deprived of God's unconditional love. And I am like everyone else on earth in this regard! All I would ever need to do would be to ASK for help from God and I would receive it. – I knew/understood that my life as Lydia was not finished, and that death is a choice. Because of the unconditional Love I received, I felt I COULD return and face anything I had remaining on my 'plate' in life."*

Candice was twenty-one when she left her body during a criminal attack in which she was choked. She reports an unconditional love: *"Suddenly, I was aware of a brilliant, shining white light ahead. The light was all encompassing, beautiful, but did not hurt my eyes. I felt incredible, unconditional, complete love permeate my being. I experienced a knowing of all the questions. At the end of the tunnel was a river that I crossed to reach a spiritual shape with outstretched arms on the other side. I knew this was the source of the light and the being was Jesus. I could hear Jesus's voice in my heart, full of acceptance and love."*

Veronika, who suffered a serious head injury in an automobile accident, returned from her near-death experience and reflected on its impact on her. She says of the unconditional love, *"What has given me the joy and peace and new understandings every day is the overwhelming, INTENSE, POWERFUL, DEEP, UNCONDITIONAL LOVE LOVE LOVE LOVE LOVE LOVE for all that was there."*

LOVE IS NON-JUDGMENTAL

Some experiencers are surprised when they discover that profound love is non-judgmental and God is not vindictive. Their accounts give examples of being loved in spite of drug and alcohol addiction, imprisonment, and other "socially unacceptable" behaviors.

Brenda awoke from an extended near-death-like dream with new understandings. She reports, *"There was no sense of retribution. In no way did I get the feeling that anything associated with God was punitive. All was love, compassion and endless opportunity to learn."*

Harrison, the inmate being treated for a pulmonary embolism, found himself in the light. He *"began to understand many things,"* and realized that *"Sin is a cultural concept which uses the fear of God's punishment to keep whole populations in line. It is impossible to sin spiritually as no soul would ever dream to cause harm to another soul. God is a God of love and does not punish."*

Sorcha, who died in the automobile accident on a visit to New Zealand, recounts a complete absence of judgment: "*With a blink of an eye, I was somewhere else, full of Love, Light and friends. Standing with me was a Light-Being, draped in transparent-light robe, flowing as if it were a part of his Light-Being. I felt amazing Peace and Love . . . A complete absence of judgments of any kind that was more euphoric than any opiate drug I had tried during my addiction years in my 'life before.'*"

Reg was a fifty-seven-year-old "*full-blown alcoholic, deep into life-threatening despair and depression*" when he had a near-death experience in which a voice warned him, "*Quit or die.*" After the near-death experience, he never so much as wanted another drink. Eight months later, he had an NDE-like experience while listening to an inspirational recording. He says, "*Someone grabbed me like you would pick up a child in two hands and put me inside a very large cathedral . . . In the center of a large empty floor was a raised dais and on the dais was an enormous ball of light that was taller than I, maybe twice as tall. I walked to the light and as I did, It extended two arms of light that embraced me. Merging with the light I knew that everything was okay, that I was not judged unworthy, and I was loved and acceptable regardless of what I had done.*"

Tabitha, who had a near-death-like dream of being with Mother Mary, says she woke up knowing that humans could do nothing to lose God's unconditional love. "*God's love is infinite and eternal and unconditional FOR EVERY ONE OF US. It doesn't matter what our religion is or if we drink or smoke or curse. It isn't dependent at all on anything we do, and we can never lose it. It is a gift from God to us forever. To ALL HIS CHILDREN everywhere."*

Gayla was forty-one when she had a near-death-like dream in which she found herself going to the light as if drawn by a magnet. Although she stopped just outside the light, she says, *"God talked to me. He was telling me things. He gave me knowledge of some of what I was to know. Things such as He is just love, and that all the teachings of Him being mean and that he was someone to fear was wrong."*

LOVE IS ALL-INCLUSIVE

Other experiencers explain that there is no favoritism in love. Despite our many theories and beliefs about who will deserve a happy afterlife, the following examples make it clear that love transcends our limited understanding.

Josephine had open-heart surgery at the age of forty-two, during which she met God and he spoke with her. She confesses to having been against all religious beliefs before experiencing that God loves everyone unconditionally. *"When I went in to the hospital I was not at all a spiritual person and was not worried about the surgery. But I came back a totally changed person. Prior to my experience I was against all types of religious beliefs. Now I have dedicated my life to God and wish to fulfill His purpose for my life. I no longer fear death and realize that it is preferable to being here. But while I am here, I would like to touch as many lives as possible and relate to them the joy and peace that can be found in God. I want to tell people how much God loves them and to have them experience the happiness that I have found."* She concludes by saying, *"I hope that I can help in some way to let others know that God has a purpose for each of us and that He loves every one of us unconditionally."*

Devin, who died in a vehicle accident, learned there is no room for religious intolerance. *"My experience on the other side taught me that there is no room there for petty things like intolerances, such as only Christians can go and meet Jesus Christ, and that only via him can one reach the other side, heaven. That this place is only for Baptists, or Mormons, Catholics, and other western type Christian based faiths to the exclusion of Buddhists, Muslims, Native Indians and the countless other flavours of spiritual beliefs. There is no intolerance whatsoever. It is and remains about love and service, that is it! The choice of whether to live with and by such a belief is very much our own choice. There is no favoritism. When I hear of people claiming they and only they have the right stuff "to enter the kingdom of heaven," I just smile quietly to myself and know that in their own time, they will know better."*

Brenda, who had a near-death-like dream, found tolerance for non-Christians. *"There was no sense that only Christians are allowed past the gate. In fact, under the circumstances, any kind of concept of ranking based on religious membership seems ridiculous. Nor was there any feeling on my part of shame, or sin, only total acceptance."*

Karola had an near-death-like dream following a miserable night of babysitting. She learned that the love she felt then is available for everyone. *"I felt nothing but love, a much higher love than anyone is capable of here on Earth. I knew that that was what gave us life while we're here, and when we go there, we'll actually be IN it."* She later noted, *"Sometimes it's the only thing that keeps me going, especially when I hear fear-mongering pastors who seem to get sadistic pleasure out of constantly threatening people with hell no matter what they do."* Finally, she concludes, *"The vision wasn't just for me, it's for everybody who wonders about heaven, or worries about it. Preachers make it too complicated. God has always reached out to us. All we have to do is receive that love, and the rest falls into place."*

Charity was being given gas during the final stages of childbirth when she left her body and had an extensive near-death experience in which she was given a tour of the universe. Later, while reflecting on her experience, she said, *"The biggest change was that I moved away from the Catholic religion of my childhood. See, one of the big things about the experience was that along with the tour I was shown the whole reason why we are here. I remember thinking that it was so simple and wondering why everyone on earth doesn't already know it, why we are still searching."* She goes on to say, *"I don't remember what it is that is so simple, but I don't think it is that the Catholic Church is the one and only way to heaven."*

Prisca was orphaned at a young age and had a hard life, filled with pain. When she was twenty-four she *"asked God, if he was real, to show me a sign of his presence and love."* The next time she did cocaine, it caused her to have two cardiac arrests and many other physical problems. After she regained consciousness in the hospital, she *"felt the most powerful, yet peaceful and serene feelings I have ever felt! I felt that I 'belonged' . . . I felt totally liberated from life's drudgeries, society's expectation, and cruel indifferences; I felt an inner connection to all of life, a realization and acceptance of accountability to myself and others. And most importantly, to not be judgmental . . . I learned there are MANY paths to God, and ALL are welcome."*

It is interesting that many experiencers come back with new spiritual understandings. Some may also change their religious affiliations. Religious people sometimes find greater tolerance for other religions or even leave their religion altogether. But others, who were not religious before their experience, have sought out religion afterwards. Many now distinguish between being spiritual and being religious.

THE WORLD OF LOVE AND LIGHT HOLDS JOY

Joy is a quality of the world of love and light that is often mentioned. Each of the people below felt joy during their near-death or near-death-like experience.

Faith had just been put under for a surgical procedure when she rose above her body. She heard a nurse telling the doctor her heart had stopped. Then she moved upward, away from her body toward a light, and heard a voice speaking to her. *"The closer I got to the voice and the light, the more love I felt, the more joy. I have never felt that experience in my life before or since. It was so beautiful."*

Alexis was twenty-nine and going through a stressful time in her life when she finally fell asleep. As she drifted off, she felt her spirit float. She soared higher and higher toward the light until she found herself in the presence of Jesus. *"I was totally filled with joy and bliss, as I have never known since, and never will know here."*

When Bert was forty-five he had an experience that profoundly changed his inner life. He was asleep in bed when he found himself in a "perfect" park-like place. *"There was the wonderful joy and loving enfolding from HIS glory, almost a 'mother's love' effect, but to the extent of permeating everything. (Note: to the extent of permeating me as well.) To intensify the joy, there was also a total absence of any negative: negative cares, negative thoughts, they simply weren't there."*

Elizabeth was sleeping peacefully when she felt herself being carried up into the dark. She looked back to see her body sleeping below as she was taken to a bright area where she saw her deceased father. He looked young again and was all dressed up. He was pacing back and forth anxiously and she understood he was awaiting her mother's arrival. *"During the whole experience there was a sense of peace, love, and joy and a powerful feeling of being at the center of knowledge."* (Elizabeth later learned that her mother had a stroke and had almost died at that time.)

Sylvanna was sleeping when her spirit joined her brother in a shared-death experience[9] at the moment the brother was killed in an automobile accident in another state. One minute she was asleep and the next she was with her brother in a tunnel, a bright light shining behind him. *"From this light I felt enormous amounts of love, freedom, joy and wellbeing that I had never felt before and I can hardly find words adequate to describe it. My brother's face was glowing and he was smiling at me and I could feel his extreme happiness."* Sylvanna awoke when the telephone rang bringing the news of her brother's fatal accident.

THE WORLD OF LOVE AND LIGHT HOLDS COMPASSION

Another quality experiencers found in the world of love and light is compassion.

Kay was a teenager when she suddenly blacked out and left her body, having become exhausted from caring for her siblings while their mother was recovering from surgery. She found herself in the light where she felt love and peace. After returning, she reported, *"I feel like I am filled with love and compassion like Jesus and God are, and I also learned from my NDE that God is compassionate, and that Love is the most important thing in this life."*

Dalles had double pneumonia when he was thirteen. He rose out of his body and saw a light coming toward him. *"I could feel a love present as the light got larger and a warmth of great compassion inside the light. There was a figure inside the light that talked to me without using words."*

THE WORLD OF LOVE AND LIGHT HOLDS ALL KNOWLEDGE

An interesting quality experiencers associate with love is unlimited knowledge. Once he arrived in the light, Tim felt "great warmth and love" and experienced "limitless knowledge." Some state that they were not able or allowed to bring back everything they learned.

Jessica, who left her body and went to the light during childbirth, says, *"There was pure love and peace in the light, and it was all knowing."*

Devin, who died in a vehicle accident, says, *"I was in a place of brilliant light. Unbelievably bright, but not hard on the eyes."* He reports, *"It was beautiful beyond imagination, seamless, infinite, there were no questions to be answered, everything was so clear and easy to understand, in fact there really was nothing to understand. I felt completely a part of this place and very much at home. I did not want to leave this place. It was a place of all power, knowledge and love."*

Marsha, who had an allergic reaction to IV dye, reports, *"I had so many questions, but they were answered as I asked them. It was very strange, like thought transference, no voices."*

Rob died at age fifteen when a speeding car hit his motorcycle, severing his left leg, breaking bones, and causing head injury. He found himself floating above the treetops, then speeding upward surrounded by an intense white light. He says, *"I was experiencing a euphoria that I can't describe. I understood everything."*

Sophie was thirty-one when she was in an accident involving head trauma. She went out of her body and said, "*I felt connected to all knowledge and had a sense of knowing about all life – past and future.*"

Lucie had a seizure from an allergic reaction to medication when she was fifty-two. She was released after several days in intensive care and had what she calls an epiphany from which, "*I can only say I emerged with a total understanding of the machinations of the universe and the phrase 'love is the answer; communication is the key.'*"

Gayla, who was forty-one when she had a near-death-like dream, found herself going to the light as if drawn by a magnet. She stopped just outside the light where God talked to her and told her many things, such as, "*That all people were good. That there were different layers in heaven and that our life on earth and how we live it determines what level we would enter Heaven. I can not remember all he told me and it kind of angers me . . . And I also seem to know I was not to remember it all as it would be too much for my brain on earth to hold or comprehend.*"

Charity, who was being given gas during the final stages of childbirth, left her body and found herself going up a dark tunnel into a glowing light at the end. She says, "*The next thing I remember, I was being given a tour, not of 'heaven' but of everything, from the whole of the universe to the smallest atom. As it was ending, my guide and I were standing in a garden and I became aware of some other being coming up to my guide. I moved away a bit because I didn't want to be eavesdropping. They conferred briefly and my guide came up to me and told me there had been a mistake and that I would have to go back. Well, saying I was deeply disappointed doesn't even begin to describe how I felt and I let my guide know it. I alternated between being angry and begging not to go. I really made a fool of myself, and all the time my guide just kept gently smiling and saying that they were sorry but I would have to, and I wouldn't remember any of this. Well, I just informed them that oh yes, I will, and what's more I'm telling everyone about it, and I proceeded to list all the names of those I intended to tell. What a jerk! That didn't faze them a bit, and they actually laughed at me."* After she returned, she remembered some things, but not everything she was shown.

Some experiencers, while not mentioning that they received all knowledge, were nonetheless told or shown fascinating details while they were in the world of love and light.

Darryl drowned when he was a nine-year-old farm boy trying to see how long he could hold his breath under water as he swam in the pond. He left his body and had many experiences in the light until his dog pulled his body from the pond. At one point in his journey, he says, *"The bright light was next for me to explore. I asked if it was God. They said I could call it that, but Creator was a better term. The light was very large, and bright golden white, with sparks or small specks of energy flying out in all directions. I had to see what made it work, so I stuck my head inside and looked around. I saw many colors, patterns, and shapes. Some years later many were recognized as DNA structures, and often I see these shapes and the geometry in just-invented devices. It was great fun."*

Avril left her body during a drug overdose when she was sixteen. She felt herself being pulled backward, then she went through a tunnel, and finally she reached the light. Following other experiences there, she says, *"At that moment I saw a ray of light with a being in it and the love from his light filled my entire being up . . . He began to talk and teach me things. The way that I was taught was a lot different though than the way you would learn here. When we communicated, it was telepathically, and he could talk to me and I could comprehend a lot faster than here on earth. He showed me past civilizations and the future of what I was a part of."*

Diane was twenty-five in 1959 when her blood pressure fell precipitously as she was preparing to give birth to her second child. She found herself in a beautiful, peaceful place filled with flowers. She reports, *"Then, someone started to talk to me. I didn't see His face. I say 'His' because it was a male voice. He said, 'Diane, I am leaving you here (on Earth) for a purpose!' He then proceeded to make known to me ALL THINGS. As He talked to me, I thought: 'Why me, as I am not anyone special; but since He has revealed all to me so clearly, now when I return back to Earth, I can help so many people.' As soon as I thought this, He answered by saying, 'No one will know what you are going through.' When He finished talking, I started to float back to Earth, and the closer I got, the dirtier and uglier it appeared. I then felt myself enter into my body on the operating table with a sound like WHOOSH!"*

THE WORLD OF LOVE AND LIGHT HOLDS PEACE

Peace is the quality most frequently associated with love. Despite the chaotic circumstances many experience prior to leaving their bodies, they often feel great peace once they are out and especially when they get into the light.

Maxine was succumbing to a raging infection in her body while in the emergency room waiting to be seen. She speaks of the peaceful silence she found. *"I kept drifting away, receding down that long dark tunnel. I felt drawn toward that peaceful silence yet fought to climb back to the surface. At one point, I awakened to find myself clawing at the air as though I were trying to climb out of a pit. In that silence was peace. It felt as though I had walked to the edge of the valley of the shadow of death. All fear was gone – there was only hope and love in abundance. I had a choice: I could stay and let the peace envelop me, or I could live on and let life excite me. You know what I chose."*

Sidney was a sophomore in college when one night, lying in bed, he found himself unable to move or make a sound. When he was able to relax, he found himself surrounded by light. He speaks of finding total peace. *"I was struck by the sheer intensity of the emotions I had while in the 'place' (as I later began to call it). There was the feeling of my being completely whole, in every sense of the meaning. And with the sensation of being complete came with it the feeling of, for the first time in my 'life', having total peace."* Later he reflects, *"Again, the feelings of complete happiness, joy, love, wholeness, and especially peace were overwhelmingly wonderful. So much so that I recall being moved to tears while there, even though I still have no recollection of a body to speak of."*

Josephine, who had open-heart surgery at the age of forty-two, felt the peace. *"I felt an incredible sense of peace, joy, and happiness. I felt the tremendous love of God and an unwavering knowledge of His existence."*

Dee, who was fourteen when she died of Rocky Mountain spotted fever, felt at peace. *"I recall feeling concern for the person I saw, then feeling confused when I realized I saw myself on the table . . . just as quickly I noticed bright, but warm and peaceful light . . . I felt overwhelming peace and love . . . I remember feeling very 'at peace,' very comforted, VERY loved, whole and complete."*

Dory had been having episodes of passing out and had a heart attack at age twenty-one. While she never left her body, she received that peace. *"My whole soul felt peace and love."*

Berenice, who slipped in the bathroom and was knocked out, was comforted with a peacefulness. *"I thought, 'Oh, it's real.' I never really believed in heaven or God. I didn't consider myself an atheist. I just never put a lot of thought into religion or talk about it."* In a moment, she says, *"I looked around and I was in a black sky, with a million stars. I am kind of claustrophobic, so I didn't get the tunnel experience. I didn't know what to think. I thought, 'Is this what happens?' As soon as I would start to be scared, a peacefulness would come over me that I have never before felt. In this place was love and peace and comfort."*

Davin, who was five when his heart stopped during corrective oral surgery, felt peace. "*I then felt myself being 'drawn' toward a source of comfort and heat. I knew it was light, yet I could not see this. I felt the beings all around me, emotionally guiding me without touch or word. I knew none of this, yet I did. This place felt like my natural home, like I belonged. I was enveloped by the warmth, and found myself alone with the being of warmth. I NEVER (to this day) have felt the acceptance, love, peace, and sensation of full existence I felt that day."*

THE WORLD OF LOVE AND LIGHT HAS NEW SOUNDS AND COLORS

Some experiencers describe sounds and colors that are beyond those found on earth. They say their senses are expanded in the world of love and light. It's hard for me to imagine a color we don't have here, but that is one of the things they report.

Melisse, who had a high fever from German measles when she was seven, closed her eyes and "*suddenly the darkness behind my eyelids got very black.*" She was approached by what she could only call a cloud. She said, "*As the cloud entered, I heard the most gorgeous sound, like millions upon millions of voices singing – no words – just beautiful interweaving of harmonies, sounds that just can't be described. I remember hearing a note so high that I thought 'Nobody can sing a note that high.' It was quite awesome.*"

Diane, whose blood pressure fell precipitously while she was preparing to give birth, reported, "*I glanced at the wall clock (I don't know why) and then suddenly I found myself in this absolutely most beautiful, peaceful place. The flowers were extraordinarily beautiful, and there was such lovely music. I can only say the flowers were so much more beautiful than any we see on Earth, and with that kind of music and beauty, and being surrounded by love and peace, I had no wish to return to Earth.*"

Davey, who died of starvation as a prisoner of war, says, "*I passed into boundless fields of beautiful flowers with a radiance unimaginable on earth. Imagine roses and all other varieties of flowers shining with a radiance of colored sunshine, vibrant, radiant, voluptuous and delicate their reds, yellows, blues and lilacs.*"

Morie, who had a heart attack, reported, "*Then the colors!! Each area of soft turbulence seemed to have it's own color. All were very bright! I noticed that from top right to bottom left seemed to separate pastels to my left from deeper colors to my right. No artist could ever come even close to copying those colors, and I have never seen anything close to them in nature. Even the most beautiful sunrise or sunset has nothing like it.*"

Simone was fifty-two when she came home exhausted and laid down feeling short of breath and sick. Several years later, after attending a workshop on near-death experiences, she began remembering what happened to her that day. She recalls, *"I was in a place of soft white light. All around me were what appeared to be beautiful wisps of colored chiffon, floating gently. It was as if I knew them, I was part of them. We were enfolded in love."*

In the next chapter, we will look at some answers to the question, "Where does love come from?" In our introductory story, we hear of several sources from which profound love emanates. Other experiencers describe additional sources from which they receive the love.

Chapter Six

Love Emanates from Many Sources

A light appeared moving gently toward me and developed into an angel . . . I was shocked, and thought, "This is crazy, I don't believe in angels." [As] his/her laughter . . . flowed through me it was pure love, understanding and knowing. – Tory

I have wondered about the source of the love that poured into me during my own mystical experience. Did it come from my guardian angel, guide, deceased father, or from God? I never knew for sure, so I directed my gratitude to God, and I felt more connected to God than I had in a long time. After hearing from near-death experiencers, I believe that God is the ultimate source of all love. I believe that being created in God's image means we are all created from love and that we can all emanate love to others.

From the time I started reading 478 near-death experiences, I wanted to know when and where love was encountered. I learned that some people feel love as soon as they leave their bodies, often from a guide who goes with them. Others begin to feel love in outer space, or in the void, or as they enter a tunnel. The greatest love is most frequently felt as soon as they arrive in the light or from beings they interact with in the light.

In our introductory experience, Tory receives love from many sources once he is out of his body. We will also hear from others who report receiving love from various entities, including from the light, God, Jesus, and from unidentified light beings. Some report receiving love from multiple sources.

TORY'S EXPERIENCE

Tory was a fifty-year-old Australian man who was caught in a vicious cycle of anger and bitterness.

I thought what happened to me couldn't possibly be a 'near death experience' because I wasn't close to death. I later found out this is still possible.

In September 1996, due to a build-up of circumstances over a ten-year period, I was suicidal . . . I was laying on my bed, needing to go to work, stuck in a situation that seemed hopeless to me. I really wanted to die, as it was the only way I could see out of the mess I was in.

In a tunnel

Suddenly I became sort of aware of a black spot at the corner of the ceiling, and instantly I was in a dark space, but aware of a spot of light at the end of it. I was in a tunnel and moving towards the light. I was intensely aware that the walls of this tunnel were of 'living blackness.' It was a warm, velvety substance . . . It was loving, warm, 'supportive/positive' – and none of these words even begin to describe this adequately . . . I also realized then that I was not in my body.

Met by an angel

A light appeared moving gently toward me and developed into an angel. Quite tall, wings, golden/white, glowing, bright – both intense to my 'eyes' and yet soft. He/she had all the usual robes, the way angels are depicted here on earth. Except the quality, affect, or radiance this angel had about it was indescribable. Just to be in the presence of this was to be part of it. There were no words, we just 'knew.' I was shocked and thought, "This is crazy, I don't believe in angels." His/her laughter was an indescribable quality that was in a sense always present, flowed out like ripples, was tangible in that as the laugh flowed through me it was pure love, understanding and knowing. I was still shocked as I thought angels 'should' be kind of serious, not happy and laughing!

To write this takes time, yet all the above happened in what seemed like an instant, yet fully deeply experienced in an impact I hadn't ever felt before. I also 'registered' that the angel was neither male nor female yet both. (You can imagine why it has been so hard to describe this.)

The angel 'told' me that if I really wished to die, I could get sick and die quite quickly. This was very matter-of-fact. This seemed attractive to me, but I thought of my son and wanted to be there (on earth) for him. This also felt impossible as I had three people on earth that I had harbored anger and resentment toward for a long time. I had been doing a lot of personal development work and yet no matter how hard I tried, I couldn't release this. I hated feeling that way, yet seemed unable to change it. I just didn't want to go back living with that obsessive, destructive anger and bitterness.

Met by Jesus

As soon as I thought/said this, a brighter spot of light was at the end of the tunnel, which seemed a long way off, yet we met almost immediately. It was blinding light. At first I couldn't 'see' (this is strange because I didn't actually have eyes), but I knew this was Jesus. This was even more of a shock as I didn't believe in Jesus either. Which also seemed 'funny.'

This quality of humor is one of the most surprising and wonderful things about my experience, and one I can remember the feel of. It is an all-loving, all-knowing, all-permeating acceptance. Again, my words don't do this justice in any way. It was like, "Yes, I exist, isn't that wonderful? I'm glad you're enjoying discovering this." I was just 'basking' in the presence of this LOVE.

Hurt, anger and bitterness removed

I seemed to be sad about going back and experiencing all the human things again, in particular the anger and bitterness. I just wanted to stay 'there.' I was asked, "Is it the anger and bitterness that stops you going back?" I answered, "Yes." Jesus seemed to move his arm towards me and yet he didn't, and a beam of light passed through 'me.' The light was both a beam (like a light-house beam) and yet from/part of him. It was as if 'someone pulled the plug out.' I felt all the hurt and anger and bitterness drain out of me, like an actual substance. I had a sense of emptying.

Shown a purpose

Next, I have a sense of having been shown what it was I had to do. A path, but I have forgotten what it is. However, when something happens in my life that is a part of that, I get the feeling that I 'know' it is connected to that. Sometimes it's even as though a hand is at my back gently supporting and moving me forward.

Return

I was feeling so empty and relieved and amazed and yet calm. I was joined by another Angel. I didn't want to go back but I knew I was going to, and that was ok. They moved with me a bit down the tunnel and then suddenly I was 'back' in my body, on my bed. I was stunned, heavy, very heavy; my body felt alien to me. Like I didn't 'fit.' It felt 'yucky' – 'dead meat' is an expression I've read and it really fits.

I was confused. What had just happened? I had some memory/knowing . . . like, there is no such thing as time (I was always living by the clock). In the cosmic sense, time does not exist. Everything is perfect! Nothing is 'wrong'. Even the greatest 'evil' to us in our limited thinking is the way it is meant to be. I tried hard to remember what I was supposed to do, but knew it was ok, it would all happen, unfold.

Then I remembered the draining! I 'felt' into myself. No anger! No bitterness! No wish for revenge! I couldn't believe it, but it was true. I thought of the worst that had happened to me. Still no anger. I scoured my mind for all the things I had been obsessing about for years; there was just peace. Incredible peace. At that instant I knew that whatever it was that had just happened to me, it had changed my life and it didn't matter what it was, it was GOOD. I just spontaneously started praying my thanks, my gratitude. The rest of the day I was scared this feeling would go away. Every time I 'tested' – no anger. I just fell to my knees and prayed my gratitude and thanks.

Now I feel I'm at the part of my life where whatever it is I'm supposed to do is near. Part of this is telling about my experience. Just to put more information out there. I guess writing it is a big step.

I am grateful that Tory wrote his experience down and sent it to IANDS. It is a beautiful expression of the world of love and light, and it shows multiple sources of love towards him.

Tory refers to the tunnel, the first angel, and Jesus as sources of love he encountered after he started moving toward the light. Here are some of the various sources of love mentioned by other experiencers.

THE LIGHT IS A SOURCE OF LOVE

The most commonly reported source of love is the light itself.

Jessica, the young woman who died during childbirth, said the love was in the light. *"There was pure love and peace in the light and it was all knowing."*

Cassandra, who drowned while innertubing, says, *"I was completely wrapped in a warm soft cloudlike light . . . It was like being wrapped in love."*

Marsha, who had an allergic reaction to IV dye, arrived in the light and found love there. *"I . . . came out into a brilliant light, comparable to nothing on this earth not even the sun, not even close."* She said she felt *"lots of love and a definite sense of being loved unconditionally."*

Charlotte had a heart attack at age forty-one and felt the love while aware of the light and a presence. *"I was then aware of nothing else but great, loving warmth, intensely bright light, and a presence."*

Kay, the teenager who blacked out from exhaustion, was enveloped in the light and felt love. *"Suddenly a small, bright light appeared far off and then it got closer to me until I was enveloped in this light. I felt so much love and peace."*

Cassie was being prepared for emergency surgery to treat a ruptured ectopic pregnancy when she left her body and found love in the light. *"I looked upwards and saw the most amazing light. It was all wonderful emotions rolled into one: love, wonder, delight, peace. I could breathe again without pain and the convulsions had stopped."*

Chloe hemorrhaged during the birth of her first child at age twenty-two. She felt a loving feeling as she approached the light. *"As I started to pass over, there was a bright light and a voice saying not to be afraid. I felt very warm and a very tender and loving feeling came over me. I was assured that I would be OK and that I would be returning to my body."*

Wilma was recovering in the hospital from a major illness when she was thirty-two. She dreamt of going to the light and says the love was radiated by the light. *"I was in a very dark place. I felt compelled to climb up a very high, difficult cliff—*

which I did, with great effort. Upon reaching the top, I came upon the most magnificent light you can imagine. It had amazing colors and it radiated love. I felt at perfect peace and harmony. There was music (like the tinkling of bells). I felt a sense of pure happiness, which went 'through' me."

Sidney, the college sophomore who left his body, was surrounded by the light and felt the love. "*The next thing I recall was being surrounded by a soft, non-threatening yellow-golden light. It was everywhere and was all encompassing . . . The feelings of complete happiness, joy, love, wholeness, and especially peace were overwhelmingly wonderful.*"

Kathleen committed suicide by taking pills. She approached a light that gave her a feeling of love. "*I felt as if I was standing at the end of a dark tunnel that approached the Kingdom doors. There was a light coming from behind the doors and wall. It was the brightest, whitest, glowing light that I had ever seen. Almost as if the sun was coming up from behind them. I remember the light was so bright but I could look right at it without it hurting my eyes. It also gave me a feeling of peace, warmth and love like I had never felt before.*"

GOD IS A SOURCE OF LOVE

Some experiencers have been told that God is the ultimate source of love. Others simply experience love coming from God.

Letty, whose heart stopped during an eclamptic convulsion the day after she gave birth, was heading toward the light. *"When I went through the ceiling I was outside in the dark. The darkness was so deep it seemed solid. It was pierced by a brilliant, blue-white light . . . and even though it was unbelievably bright it did not hurt to look at it. I was drawn to the light . . . The closer I came to that light, the more overwhelmed I was by beauty, love, and peace . . . I knew God was behind that light, and I wanted to go into it with all my being."*

Kathryn was in labor at the age of twenty and had received an epidural for pain when she felt she was fading away. She popped out the top of her head and found herself in total darkness, traveling *"at light speed . . . in a cylinder-like tunnel . . . Then the next thing I remember is the travel ending and I was embraced by a bright white light. I floated peacefully in the whiteness. Feeling wonderful joy. I felt love, then I realized the light was God and that I was one with the Light."* When she remembered she was giving birth, Kathryn says, *"I knew that I had to go back and that everything would be okay. 'Remember the Light and the Peace and the Love and the Joy. Carry it with you.' Those are the messages that I received simultaneously and understood. I did not hear them. I felt them! I knew them! Just as I knew that my child would be a healthy girl. (I had not had a sonogram)."* Fifteen minutes after waking up back in her body, she gave birth to a baby girl.

Cass had an illegal abortion, crudely performed, in 1968 when she was thirty-five, and was in excruciating pain when her friend took her to the emergency room. Before they arrived, she knew she was dying. "*All of a sudden, I felt myself lifted out of my body. I did not look down at myself, in fact, I don't remember looking anywhere. But the feeling was as though I was being taken into the arms of God, a concept I had never considered. Every sorrow, all grief, heartbreak, disappointment, loss, resentment was gone. It was simply handled. Period. I then felt the most unbelievable love, mercy, and peace that I could ever imagine. In fact, one can't imagine it; it simply doesn't exist on this plane of consciousness. There are no words to describe it, and so I just have to 'know' it. It was the greatest gift I have ever known.*"

Fiona drowned in 1964 when she was five, on a family trip to the ocean. "*The next thing I remember I awoke in a cold, dark, cave-like tunnel. I was scared, confused, and freezing. As I arose, I could see in the distance some sort of light. As I moved toward the comforting light, I felt an indescribable sense of God's love and security, of utmost peace and acceptance. Everything was going to be fine.*"

Natalie was seven and a half years old when she learned to astral travel, and one night she went fast and far outside her body. "*I heard a woman's voice say in the most gentle voice I have ever heard, 'Far enough child!' and then a Light came from where I perceived the voice came from . . . Before I could get my bearing, I saw a woman come out of the Light and then I asked, 'Who are you?' and she said gently 'God.' And I thought about how it was that Jesus was supposed to be God and this was a woman! So I said, 'Naaahhhh.' And she said, in an incredibly gentle voice, 'Uh huh.' And I just knew she was. Then she asked me if I would like to sit on her lap and I thought, 'Golly, I better do it because I might never get another chance like this.' And so I did and we talked about a bunch of stuff."*

Kathie, who became ill while riding in the back seat of a car with friends, left her body and traveled through space. After she arrived in the light, she said, *"I suddenly realized that the 'God' I had been presented wasn't anything like the reality. I saw that it doesn't matter if you call him God, Allah, Great Spirit or whatever, He is the same thing. The different religions just have different ways of explaining the same Creator. I also realized that little voice inside us that prompts us to do good things comes from this Creator. It is that Light of Love inside each of us."*

Each of the experiencers in this section feels love coming from a source they describe as God. But they all experience God in different ways. Although many refer to God as male, Natalie experienced God as female. I have heard of several others who were invited to sit on God's lap, but they experienced God as a man, usually with white hair and a beard. Some encounter God as a ball of light, and some don't perceive any form at all. After reading many accounts, I have concluded that God can appear in any form God wishes, according to what is appropriate for the person. Most people who experience God simply "know" it is God, and don't need to be told.

JESUS IS A SOURCE OF LOVE

Tory found that prior belief in Jesus was not necessary to receive his love. Here are other experiencers who received love from Jesus.

When Marilyn was twenty-six, she was home alone with her two-year-old son and began feeling ill. Her heart sped up and she fell to the floor, unable to breathe. She says, *"My vision went black. I saw a hole open up. I went through a dark tunnel toward a light. The passage of time in the tunnel was very rapid. I did not feel frightened. When I reached the light, I was embraced by Christ and felt unconditional love. He had a warm feeling (hard to describe) and he glowed with light that was bright but did not hurt my eyes. He showed me a landscape that had flowers, trees and colors that I had never seen on earth. Everything seemed larger, and there was no shadow. He let me know that I had to go back. I wanted to stay. The next thing I knew, I was beginning to awake. I have regretted to this day that I regained life. I wish I had been able to stay. I know that sounds funny, but that's how I feel."*

Fernando was thirty-two and had pain down his left arm for a week before having a heart attack in his sleep. He awoke looking down on himself and his wife in bed. *"I was out of my own body . . . I felt so peaceful and happy like if I had let go of a heavy weight. I was moving so fast. I saw a light I was on the way to. When I got to that light all my life came in front of me like a fast movie.*

Everything was there, all my life. I went into that beautiful light. It was too bright. No words are possible to try to tell somebody about it. I started seeing people but they were people of light. I cannot explain them any other way . . . Suddenly from that light emerged a person that I realized immediately was our Lord Jesus Christ. I looked at him and he looked at me with so much love. I tried to tell him how happy I was there in that exact moment but I tried to tell him that I also had a son and I would like to see him grow up. It's like words weren't necessary. I came back inside my body again. I breathed very deeply and I felt my body warming up and life again in it."

Candice, who was twenty-one when she was attacked and choked, felt her essence leave her body and float above it and was surprised but not distraught or concerned. She went through a dark tunnel. *"Suddenly, I was aware of a brilliant, shining white light ahead. The light was all encompassing, beautiful, but did not hurt my eyes. I felt incredible, unconditional, complete love permeate my being. I experienced a knowing of all the questions. At the end of the tunnel was a river. I could feel the water as I crossed to reach a spiritual shape with outstretched arms on the other side. I knew this was the source of the light and the being was Jesus. I could hear Jesus's voice in my heart, full of acceptance and love. He asked if I wanted to stay or return. I was pregnant with my son, but there was such a longing to stay encompassed by the feeling of complete love. I answered, 'I must go back for my son.' I immediately returned to my body on the floor."*

Rina was running a high fever from pneumonia, was taken to the hospital, and left her body. *"I was floating through darkness and I saw a bright white figure that was absolutely glowing and beautiful. I went toward this beautiful being and realized all at once that I was standing before Jesus Christ. The love that I felt at that moment was indescribable. I knew that I was in the presence of our Lord. He reached out to me with His right hand and touched me on the left shoulder. He didn't speak with his mouth, but I got the message that he was healing me and sending me back because it wasn't my time yet. He showed me images of my children and I knew that was why I was going back. The next thing I knew, I was waking up in the hospital bed."*

Alexis, who was going through a stressful time in her life, felt her spirit float as she drifted off to sleep. She flew higher and higher and the light became stronger until she found herself in the presence of Jesus. *"I bowed down and said 'Lord, Lord of all the world I am not worthy of your presence' . . . He spoke to me of many things, some I cannot remember now but it mostly went like this: 'You are my special child and I have loved you always.' Jesus then waved his hand and showed me my family – husband and two little boys aged two and five. I saw and 'knew' them differently – loving them, but as other souls I have known before. I felt so safe and loved I did not want to return."*

AN UNIDENTIFIED BEING IS A SOURCE OF LOVE

Tory received love from an angel. Here are cases where the identity of the being radiating the love is not known. Some refer to a light being or being of light. Others refer to a guide, angel, monk, figure, etc.

Dawn, who was delivering twins by C-section when she left her body, was met by an unidentified being. *"A being that was behind me and to my left said, 'Come with me.' I tried to turn to see this being but 'he' stayed just within my peripheral vision. I knew he was tall. The feeling of safeness and love that came over me at the second he spoke was incredible. This feeling defies explanation. He guided me . . . upward through the roof of the hospital."*

Agatha, who remembers extreme pain and going in and out of her body as she was being born, was with a figure full of light and love. *"I looked up and out through the back of my head up a long dark fluid pipe that curved up towards a doorway. As I was looking I was drawn back up there and felt no pain. I was with a figure in the doorway. The figure was full of light and movement. The doorway held the same kind of light. I knew this figure knew me more than anyone ever would know me, both good and bad, and accepted me and loved me. The light was in constant motion and even though it was bright, it was wonderful to look at. It felt warm and loving. It was familiar and safe for me."*

Charity, who was being given gas during the final stages of childbirth, left her body. *"I found myself going up a dark tunnel, not completely black, with a glowing light at the end. When I arrived, I saw glowing beings waiting for me and the most loving, accepting, glorious Presence greeting me. This Presence was so awesome and so intimate all at once, and was so happy to see me. But I didn't get the feeling that it was God."*

Rowena was a thirty-five-year-old Jewish woman driving home from her business in Australia when her car hydroplaned and hit a pole. She was in a coma for ten days. She left her body and headed for the light. *"I rushed greedily forward towards this light. I arrived in an explosion of glorious light into a room with insubstantial walls, standing before a man about in his 30's, about 6 foot tall, reddish brown shoulder length hair and an incredibly neat short beard and mustache. He wore a simple white robe, light seemed to emanate from Him and I felt He had great age and wisdom. He welcomed me with great Love, tranquility, Peace (undescribable), no words. I felt "I can sit at your feet forever and be content," which struck me as a strange thing to think/say/feel. I became fascinated by the fabric of His robe, trying to figure out how light could be woven!"*

After a life review, Rowena met her grandfather. *"He looked younger than I remembered and was without his harelip or cleft pallet, but undoubtedly my grandfather. We hugged. He spoke to me and welcomed me . . . Granddad told me that Grandma was coming soon and he was looking forward to her arrival. I enquired why she was coming soon as she had been traveling from her home in Manchester to New Zealand to Miami for continual summer for a number of years! Granddad told me she had cancer of the bowel and was coming soon. (Grandma was diagnosed 3 months later and died in August)."* Rowena's report of meeting her grandfather illustrates the fact that deceased loved ones on the other side appear in their prime and in good health. Her grandfather no longer had his harelip.

Lynn, who drowned when she was five, sped toward *"a point of brilliant light in the distance . . . When I reached the point of light I found myself in a world of light . . . In the midst of the light, stood a male figure. It was radiating this light, and radiating this totally unearthly complete unconditional Love. I was embraced by this being, or enveloped in its light, which felt like an embrace."*

LOVE COMES FROM MULTIPLE SOURCES

Just as Tory received love from multiple sources, so do some of the others.

Daniela was twenty-one when she began having episodes of what she calls sleep paralysis, with crushing pain in her chest. One night, she felt herself sinking down inside her own body, sucked through a cold narrow passage and becoming microscopic. She traveled at the microscopic level, losing her fear and receiving untold knowledge. *"All of a sudden, the universe of the microcosm became the universe of the macrocosm. The two of them were a continuum. The universe is infinite because it is a continuous cycle . . . I was floating through this universe feeling this overwhelming feeling of love from all the spirits that are in all things. Even the smallest speck in the universe is important in God's eyes because we are all fragments of God seeking reunification. Then I saw this light like nothing I have experienced on earth, the brightest light ever, yet it does not blind you. I wanted to be reunited with that light forever. I knew I would never tire from it; its love was everlasting.*

"As I approached the light I felt the presence of Jesus; He was the light, except he was Jesus to me because it was the most familiar thing I could associate him with. His love was so complete and unconditional. I yearned to go to him. Although I had had a very happy life, coming back to life was as attractive to me as for a human to become a roach. I had gone through a metamorphosis and now I could not go back.

"All of a sudden I was told that I had to go back because my parents had already lost my sister a couple of years earlier. I protested but I felt the most intense feeling of understanding and love; I had to obey, not out of fear but because of the love I felt for my creator; I could not doubt his wisdom. I returned to my body much faster but retracing everything, even the cold tunnel."

Daniela reports some of the changes that occurred after her return. *"In the months that followed I felt this overwhelming love towards strangers in the street; I could feel their emotions, I felt nostalgic for their memories. I felt this tremendous connection towards anything alive, and the whole universe is alive."*

Walt, who was being treated for depression by breathing a high-oxygen mixture when he went out of his body, speaks of finding himself on the roof of the building and having a life review. "*Next the tunnel, traveling down at great speed and the loving light with me. A period of darkness with glowing light surrounding me then on past what was the brightest all powerful force which I knew to be the creator. I found myself in what appeared to be a large room and in the corner was a shadowy figure which seemed to be the Christ, yet we knew one another and had a common bond of love.*"

Livie, who believes her experience was the result of a cardiac arrest following a night of drinking and drugs, says, "*About 2/3 of the way up the tunnel, a light being, or ball of light, came from the right wall of the tunnel. This being (from here on called 'he' for convenience sake) was a loving warm light. I began to make an act of worship by kneeling and he stopped me, but not by physical means and not by normal language communication, I can't really say how that happened . . .*

"*At the end of the tunnel . . . I felt the loving warm light even more intensely and found myself in a 'place' of warm loving light . . . I looked up and it was as if he stood behind me and took my shoulders and turned me to my right and then remained just behind me and to my right. It was as if he was presenting me to the Source of the loving warm light which was the 'center' of the light. I raised my arms to the light and said 'Oh Jesus, you feel so good!' which although spoken aloud was not by physical means . . . The loving warm light got more intense and I was embraced or absorbed (for lack of a better word) into this Source.*

"*Although all of my experience is extremely difficult to describe this is the most 'ineffable' part of it. The word 'bliss' does not do it justice. I was 'released' and looked to the left and then was 'embraced' by Greg, a family friend who had died of AIDS. I really didn't see Greg, but only another being of light much like the one I met in the tunnel. I just knew it was Greg. I experienced his essence. He was one with the Source for he too reflected the Source's loving warm light. It was as if I 'melded' with Greg. I then faced the Source or Center of the light and my head was turned to my right and I fell away, but I don't remember actually falling. The next thing I know is that I woke up."*

Livie's encounter with Greg brings to mind the concept that, on the other side, people are not necessarily recognized by their appearance or because they tell us their name. We recognize them by sensing their energy signature, or what Livie calls their essence. I have concluded that when an experiencer identifies the being they are encountering, it is because they spontaneously recognize that being's unique energy signature.

In the next chapter, we address the question, "Are we really all interconnected?" The introductory experience points to that understanding, and we will see what information others bring back from the world of love and light about the concept that we are all part of the one source, that love is our essence, and that we are never alone.

Chapter Seven

We Are All One and Love Is Our Essence

We are each to love and care for any and every life we come in contact with because we are all a part of the One God, the Universe: we are all a living part of the same living being, and subsequently, we are all a part of each other!
– Miles

I was introduced to the concept that we are all one a long time ago, but I still have a hard time grasping this concept fully. Now that I have heard near-death experiencers talk about our interconnectedness, my desire is even greater to know what this feels like. Likewise, when near-death experiencers say that love is our essence, I struggle to integrate this teaching. I understand that love is God's essence, but it adds a whole new dimension for me to learn that love is our essence also. Related to our interconnectedness is the concept reported by experiencers that we are never alone.

In our introductory account, we hear from Miles. Of Lebanese/American heritage, Miles was only twenty-three when a blood vessel burst in his head while he was driving. He doesn't remember the resulting accident or going out of his body, but he does remember being shown things that changed his worldview while he was unconscious. Miles learned that everything created is connected and part of a greater whole and that we are to love and care for each other.

MILES'S EXPERIENCE

I had headaches for months before my 'stroke,' but I paid no attention to them because I had lost all of my self esteem and feelings of self worth. I had always believed in 'God,' being brought up in the Orthodox Catholic/Eastern Catholic faith, and was always praying --- talking with God about my life and lack of direction . . . I had a brain aneurysm, a thalamic bleed, which according to my doctors should have killed me. But I survived a subsequent car accident due to the rupture and bleed which I don't even remember. I remember asking God to take my life and keep me from hurting myself and others around me, as I have in the past.

Shown we are each part of the one God

Well, I saw/was shown things that changed my views of my life and of this world that I remember choosing not to remember in detail for fear of upsetting some order of things to come. I was shown that God, in whatever form He is worshiped, EXISTS and cares for each and every one of us, without condition! And that the most important thing that we can do while we are on this planet is to care for each and every one that we can. We are all responsible for each other, because we are truly, in every sense of the notion, ONE IN GOD. We are each a part of the ONE GOD and are aware of Him in many different ways. The most simple way to understand Him is to think of Him AS the Universe. God 'the Father' is everything that we can see, touch, etc. That which we call 'Heaven' exists.

I know that what I have been shown, by powers greater than anything I have previously known, is the greatest truth that there is. Jesus Christ even said it, "Love thy neighbor as thy self!" We are each to love and care for any and every life we come in contact with because we are all a part of the One God, the Universe: we are all a living part of the same living being, and subsequently, we are all a part of each other! How can we go on hating our fellow man and causing death, grief, and destruction? We are only destroying ourselves.

Shown his purpose

I have definite knowledge of there being Life after what we now call death. As a result of my doubting my own future, I was shown that I have a purpose – but at my choosing. I will not remember, directly, what that purpose is, for fear of changing my future.

For Miles, this powerful experience resulted in new beliefs which are out of keeping with those he had before it happened. One of his new beliefs is that we are all part of the One.

In this chapter, we will hear from other experiencers who report the oneness of all creation. We will also listen to experiencers who say that love is our essence and that we are never alone.

WE ARE ALL ONE

Miles's description of the oneness of all existence is a powerful one. Other experiencers also attempt to convey the oneness of everything. Those who say they merge with the divine report, interestingly, that they don't lose their individuality in the process.

Helen, who had the life changing experience following meditation, reported, *"We are all a part of this LOVE. We are all ONE with GOD."*

Donny was eleven years old when he was put to sleep to have two teeth pulled. During the procedure, he left his body, much to the dismay of the dentist and anesthesiologist. He described what he discovered. *"In this place I felt all love, all acceptance, all forgiveness, all belonging, and reverence for the whole universe in its simple complexity. Heaven is a sea of souls, God the pool, each one a drop of water, all connected, all separately aware, but as one."* Donny was also given information about the future of the earth. He said, *"I know mankind is about to evolve to a higher consciousness and become slightly more collective. I know 'others' are interested in this because they are also collective and can no longer function effectively as individuals, so we are of great interest during the change."*

Sidney, who realized one night that he couldn't move or make a sound, left his body and learned, *"We are all a part of something much larger, and not just some simple species on an insignificant planet. We also have no right to place ourselves on a pedestal and say that nothing else is as important as ourselves. All things in this and all Universes and Dimensions are very special and significant."*

Prisca, who had a cardiac arrest while using cocaine, reports, *"I felt an inner connection to all of life, a realization and acceptance of accountability to myself and others. And most importantly, to not be judgmental."*

Sophie, who was in an accident involving head trauma, says, *"I felt connected to a powerful source—a oneness which is spiritual and more real than this bodily existence."*

Sorcha, who died in the automobile accident on a visit to New Zealand, explains, *"The life beyond . . . is a joyous one filled with indescribable Love, Peace and Forgiveness that permeates your very being, connecting you to ALL. All there ever was, is and ever will be and ALL the possibilities that lie in between. All is One. One is LIFE/LOVE."*

Joan, who was experiencing extreme grief following the death of her husband and left her body, says, *"I understood that we are all One. We are all connected, not just in a philosophical, systemic sense, but also in a very real, material (atomic?) sense. And not just people, but everything. Everything in the universe(s)."*

LOVE IS OUR ESSENCE

Miles says we all are a part of the one God, and that God is everything we can see, touch, etc. In talking about the love of which we are all a part, other experiencers emphasize that love is our true essence and at the core of our being.

Helen, the woman who returned from meditation with new knowing, said, *"This DIVINE LOVE was in everything and in me. At the core of my being I was this LOVE and so was everyone else."*

Tim, who died from an allergic reaction, put it this way: *"Our true state of existence is one of pure energy, one where time has no meaning or relevance. We have no limits, boundaries, and few rules. It is a state of pure energy, bliss and love."*

Walt, who was being treated for depression by breathing a high-oxygen mixture, shares, *"To me this was the greatest gift of the whole experience, knowing that Love and our souls are one."*

Jessica, who was twenty-six and giving birth to her daughter when she left her body, made this discovery: *"I realized too that love should be a force we feel for ourselves. We should love ourselves, embrace ourselves, and take joy in our own creation, because we are of God and part of God, who is love."*

Kathie, who went out of her body while riding in the back seat of a car due to heart problems, says, *"I also realized that little voice inside us that prompts us to do good things comes from this Creator; it is that Light of Love inside each of us."*

Lynn, who drowned at age five, explains: *"This love was all around me, it was everywhere, but at the same time it was also me, the one I was, my innermost essence."*

WE ARE NEVER ALONE

Some experiencers report that no one can ever be truly alone, since we are all part of the One and we always have someone loving us and watching over us, whether we can sense them or not.

Kit, who bled to death after an emergency C-section, says, *"The light 'told' me I had never been alone, that I had always been loved and will always be loved no matter what."*

Agatha, who remembers extreme pain and going in and out of her body as she was being born, met a being she speaks of as a "figure." She says, *"The figure told me that it would be all right. I would be okay; it reassured me that it loved me and that it was right there and would always be right there."*

Sorcha, who died in the car accident while traveling in New Zealand, had been driving on a lonely road with her daughter. Her daughter was thrown from the car, and Sorcha saw angels helping her daughter. She says, *"I heard my daughter call for help into a lone bush, growing on the edge. I begged to be allowed to return; my daughter was alone and needed me. 'She is never alone. Nobody is ever alone. I am always present, not always noticed.' The Light-Being told me, 'LOOK.' I watched as two angels appeared behind her. They took on the human form of a young white woman and a young Maori man in a suit and gold-rimmed glasses. They just appeared, with no visible means of transport. My robed Light-Being thought/told me that they were my daughter's guardian angel and a helper angel. They would protect her."*

Sidonia, who left her body during a minor outpatient surgical procedure, was shown many things by Jesus before being sent back to her body. She relates, *"Oh yea, before I left my blissful place with him, he told me to stop. At that moment all thoughts seem to halt. All I could feel was his presence. He said 'FEEL ME NOW. Even when you think I'm not there I will be here just like now.' I could feel him in every fiber of my body. I still stop sometimes just to feel his presence."*

In the next chapter, a poignant story begins to answer the question, "What is our purpose on earth?" Others will also share their experiences and understanding that we all have a purpose on earth and that learning to love is one of our primary purposes.

Chapter Eight

There Is a Reason and Purpose for Everything

> *The most difficult question I had to find an answer to during my deep searching was why we have to suffer here on earth. I now think that it is a part of the lesson we need to learn. To learn to love, sacrifice, feeling pain and loss are part of the journey of life. These experiences make us all-knowing so that we can become part of and equal to God.*
>
> – *Jessica*

I have asked God for most of my life what my purpose here is. Now that I have heard from many near-death experiencers that we all have a purpose, I am more convinced than ever that I do have one (or more than one). Only since the age of fifty have I begun to see threads in my life that have come together to help me fulfill the purpose I now believe I have. And, ultimately, no matter what form my purpose takes, I now believe we are here to learn about love and to love.

Jessica was a twenty-six-year-old woman trying to give birth when she couldn't take the pain any longer. What happened next took this young woman on an amazing journey from which she returned just in time for her daughter to be born. It wasn't until later, while searching for answers following the tragic death of her sister, that she gained new understanding about what happened to her and about her purpose on earth.

From Jessica's story, we will see that she learned that there is a reason for everything, even suffering. She came to the realization that she has a purpose to complete on earth. Some experiencers learn that we choose our lives here, and a few report we can choose additional lifetimes. More than a few agree that learning to love is the ultimate purpose of life.

JESSICA'S EXPERIENCE

One day in 1977, I had the two most incredible experiences of my life. That day I gave birth to a beautiful baby girl. On that day I also had a near-death experience!

Jessica explains that she had been in excruciating labor for thirteen hours and the pain had become unbearable. Although she begged for something to ease the pain, the nurses refused to give her medication and encouraged her to breathe deeply. The pain had become so great she felt like she was being torn in two.

Suddenly, I came up with the solution to my dilemma. I thought to myself, "I'll just will myself to die!" It seemed like such a logical solution; the only solution. When I made the decision to die I felt myself growing cold as the pain starting easing slowly. I did not start losing consciousness but instead became hyper-aware of the sights and sounds around me. Although my eyes were closed, I seemed to be able to see! The pain completely left and a wonderful feeling of relief and happiness enveloped me.

Into the light

Then to my amazement, I started drifting up from the operating table. I felt that I was in my body, but it was a different body, incredibly light and free. My other body was on the table, surrounded by doctors and nurses, but I was totally uninterested in what they were doing to it. Instead, I was intensely interested in the fact that my new body was moving higher and higher, and within a few moments I reached the ceiling. A golden-white light from above began enveloping me. Even though it was extremely bright, it was not harsh. I felt that I was going to a place that was familiar and so incredibly beautiful that I would never, never want to leave it. There was pure love and peace in the light and it was all-knowing. I felt the presence of a being but had no name for it. At the time words didn't matter anyway. I was happier than I had ever been.

I felt no regrets at all over dying. It was as if my life on earth had come and gone in an instant. All the pain, suffering, and confusion were gone. I wasn't even sad that I wouldn't see the baby I had been trying to give birth to minutes before. The light was all that mattered.

Return to her body

All of a sudden, with almost a whooshing sensation, I zapped back into my body. I was confused and angry because I wanted to stay up where the light was, not come back to a world of pain where nothing made sense, but I had no choice. The doctors finally gave me pain medication and I quickly gave birth to a healthy baby.

Jessica says she didn't mention her experience to anyone except her husband. *"Since we couldn't understand it, we spoke of it no more."* A few years later, she read Raymond Moody's book, *Life After Life,* and realized she had had a near-death experience. She read many books about NDEs but her experience didn't have much impact on her life until tragedy struck.

Dealing with devastation

Twenty years after my NDE, I had the most devastating experience of my life. On that day, my beautiful, gentle, little sister died in a horrible, tragic, senseless way. When I heard the terrible news on the phone I crumbled into a heap of pain so terrible that words can't describe it. The following days and weeks were almost unbearable. Only those who have known such grief can understand it.

I went deep within myself for an answer to why such a terrible thing could happen. I began to think again about my near-death experience and spent many hours alone, meditating. I tried to feel again what I had felt that day, and also tried to understand where my sister now was. After months of deep inner searching and questioning I began to comprehend.

New understandings

When I nearly died that day long ago, I believe I was going up to God, the source of all that was and will be, the place that we all come from and go to. The most important realization I came to is that the force of the universe is love, and that those who truly love will be with their loved ones forever. The love I have for my sister will be what joins us together for eternity. I realized too that love should be a force we feel for ourselves. We should love ourselves, embrace ourselves, and take joy in our own creation because we are of God and part of God, who is love.

We are all courageously traveling this earthly road, a road filled with pain, loneliness and confusion, even for the luckiest among us. We will all have to suffer to some extent, see loved ones die, have hopes and dreams shatter, and eventually die ourselves. Yet most of us put on a brave smile each morning and do our best to find meaning in the day. We should love ourselves for our courage.

Why do we have to suffer?

The most difficult question I had to find an answer to during my deep searching was why we have to suffer here on earth. I now think that it is a part of the lesson we need to learn. To learn to love, sacrifice, feeling pain and loss are part of the journey of life. These experiences make us all-knowing so that we can become part of and equal to God.

I have recently decided to tell about my near-death experience to anyone who wants to listen, and I fear to some who don't want to listen. I finally told my family members in hopes that they will be comforted in the knowledge that my sister is in the golden light, embraced by God, and that she is happy. The world is full of the walking wounded, those who have lost loved ones, been deeply hurt, are lonely and afraid. Perhaps sharing my experience will ease their burden somewhat.

I have become involved with the local hospice group in my town, and look forward to telling those who are getting ready to make their final transition about my experience. A wonderful opportunity was given to me when I had my near-death experience. I've been given the chance to share what I learned with others and hopefully give them the comfort of knowing that there is indeed a wonderful place for us beyond this life. It is a beautiful place where all those who have loved will go.

While the first part of Jessica's experience was a near-death experience, she later found additional profound understanding from meditation and inner searching. Thank you, Jessica, for digging deep within yourself to find these answers and for sharing them with us.

EVERY LIFE HAS A PURPOSE

During Jessica's soul-searching following her sister's death, she began to receive answers about the purpose of suffering and the purpose of life. Although Jessica was not told why she had to return to her body, and was angry and confused when she did, most experiencers say they were sent back because they had a purpose to fulfill. Let's hear what others have to say about purpose.

Josephine, who crossed over during open-heart surgery, shares, *"I remember being told that it was not yet my time to die and that I had something that I still had yet to do."*

Jinny died during an emergency hysterectomy from an allergic reaction to penicillin. She says, *"My grandmother . . . told me I had to go back. That I had a purpose that hadn't yet been met. That there were important things I had yet to learn and do before I could stay there with her. I didn't want to go. I pleaded and begged that she not send me back. But she said I had to."*

Cassandra, who drowned while innertubing in Texas, knows she was sent back for a purpose. *"There is a knowledge that I was sent back to do something else here on earth."*

Kathie, who was riding in the back seat of a car when she went out of her body due to heart problems, reports, *"I said I want to stay. I was then told that the people I was with as well as my mother would not understand and it would hurt them deeply. I understood . . . The next thing I knew, I was sitting in the back seat of the car."*

Kathryn, who went out of her body during childbirth, had a realization. *"I suddenly remembered that I had a daughter being born, and I knew that I had to go back and that everything would be okay."*

Sophie, who was in an accident involving head trauma, says, *"I believe that I experienced who I truly am – my higher self and its purpose . . . I felt loved, understood, powerful and meaningful . . . I felt a most important purpose to my being both here and 'there.' I experienced a moment of clarity which is living without fear or judgment and how important it is to find this in ourselves – to be who we truly are . . . I am concerned now about whether I am truly living up to my purpose and true self . . . I wish I could be more sure that I am doing all that I can to fulfill my purpose and to be helpful to all others."*

Karola, who had a near-death-like dream, says, *"I knew then that my life meant so much more, and was going a lot further than the superficial success the world teaches. I also knew that someday I would go there permanently . . . It was like He was giving me this [experience] as a comfort and a promise for the future . . . I now know I have to play my part in contributing to this world like everybody else. I have to fulfill my mission before I can take the heavenly reward. It was unspoken, but I've lived long enough where I can tell what it is I'm supposed to do. God wants me to use my talents for Him, to help people get beyond this world and know Him. To give them the hope I have. And the worse this world gets, the more important that is."*

Berenice, who slipped and knocked herself out, remembers, *"The being of light . . . definitely had masculine qualities . . . I keep calling it "It," because it was a light, not just a light, but the most beautiful, compassionate, wonderful being . . . It thought thoughts to me that made me realize that I needed to make the decision to return, it was not my time . . . I still wouldn't go. It seemed to be my decision to make, but It was going to see to it that I chose to come back. Then It showed me a huge 'TV screen' in the sky. On the TV screen was my two year old daughter. Just her face. It was a moving picture. I knew that I would go back to her because It had seen through me. And I did. As soon as I decided to go back, I could hear people around me. I was waking up."*

Some experiencers say they learned the purpose of life on earth, or were shown their own personal future, but don't remember what it was. Some remember, as later incidents occur in their lives, that those incidents are part of the purpose they were shown.

Donny, who was eleven when he was given anesthesia to have teeth pulled, says, *"I was 'as a courtesy' asked if I wanted to stay or go, the answer already cast in stone. I then knew I had some very important business to attend to. The world was going to change and I was going to play a part in it. I would not be allowed to know the plan until the time it started. I remembered all I was to do and was excited to be going back. I told them so. That I was going to share all this knowledge and glorious love with all back in my life. I was informed lovingly as a child that I would not be able to remember most of what I was knowing . . . I did bring some knowledge back with me."*

Charity, who was being given gas during the final stages of childbirth, says, *"I was shown the whole reason why we are here. I remember thinking that it was so simple and wondering why everyone on earth doesn't already know it, why we are all still searching. The guides were right about that one; I don't remember what it is that is so simple."*

Sorcha, who was in the automobile accident in New Zealand, says, *"The clouds rolled back again to reveal messages and scenes of my future. I was told that the information would be 'time-released' (and they are), that I would know what I need to know when I need to know it."*

Tory, who left his body during an intense desire to die, said, *"Next I have a sense of having been shown what it was I had to do. A path, but I have forgotten what it is. However, when something happens in my life that is a part of that, I get the feeling that I 'know' it is connected to that. Sometimes it's even as though a hand is at my back gently supporting and moving me forwards."*

WE CHOOSE OUR LIFE ON EARTH

Some experiencers report that we choose our life on earth. This helps explain that some of the tragedies and suffering we face were chosen by us to help us grow and serve.

Prisca, who had a cardiac arrest while using cocaine, says, *"I learned we are all here of our own accord and choosing, with a purpose to help us learn, grow and love the best we can. To serve God, by striving to return to God, in serving my fellow beings and forming the best relationships I possibly can."*

Lynn, who drowned when she was five, reports, *"I was told that it wasn't my time, that I'd been granted a visit 'back home,' but that I had to fulfill my purpose and do the work I myself had chosen to do on earth."*

Didier, who drowned during an accident at sea, says, *"What came through the strongest in these . . . experiences is that we all choose the path we are on for the potential of growth and evolvement. We all have access to God's light and love, we just need to stop, listen, and be open to it, and finally that we all have obstacles and experiences that we must overcome and learn from so that we can evolve and grow. God hasn't abandoned us when things seem tough. It is necessary to experience what we perceive as good and bad in order to grow. God's light and love is a part of each of us and we don't have to go searching for it. We just need to open up to it."*

WE MAY CHOOSE MORE LIFETIMES

When I first heard people talk about reincarnation, I could only respond by saying that it was outside my personal experience. Then, during a retreat, I was offered some regressions and surprisingly experienced two past lives. In one I died as a nobleman and in the other I was a court jester who was stoned to death. Even after my own regressions, I wasn't sure what to believe. Now, having heard from many near-death experiencers, I accept the reality of additional lives. Here are a few reports from experiencers who talk about additional earthly lifetimes.

Letty, whose heart stopped during an eclamptic convulsion after giving birth, left her body and was drawn up toward the light. She woke up the next day back in her body. She shares, *"The most unusual aftereffect of the experience is that I believe in reincarnation. I can remember my past lives and I can sometimes sense the past lives of others."* With the help of a psychologist friend, she came to understand that *"when a person undergoes an NDE and crosses the barrier between life and death, the barriers in our minds that do not allow us to remember past lives are weakened and past life memories emerge."*

Harrison had been an inmate in a state prison for sixteen years when he was treated for a pulmonary embolism and suddenly found himself *"within a totally different place which we have come to think of as heaven."* At one point while he was there, he started thinking about those he left behind. When he thought of a friend, he wanted *"to erase all difficulties from her life."* But he says, *"This was discouraged. To do so would not help her, but prevent her from learning from her own life's experiences and may have caused her to be born back into this life again."*

Brenda, who awoke from an extended near-death-like dream, gained the understanding that *"People are given opportunities to learn about and receive the graces from God. If they are not successful, they are given additional opportunities (lifetimes). There was no sense of retribution (i.e., come back to some miserable existence as punishment)."*

Jules received revelations after many years of drug addiction. He explains what was revealed to him about additional lifetimes. *"The common thread is Love. We are all heavenly spirits whose purpose in this realm is to love and to learn. There are so many lessons, too many for such a short lifetime as this. We live and learn, again and again. Sometimes we come back for the same lessons several times, until we really learn, to the soul. Sometimes we get a bunch in one shot. This is what I think happened in my case. All of our lessons are centered around God's Love. When we have learned, understood, and fully absorbed each one, we are able to help others reach the same level of understanding. Teaching is helping to understand. We all must truly learn for ourselves."*

Tim, who died in his home from an allergic reaction, saw many different lifetimes comprising his true self. *"I recall seeing my true self. I recall being at the centre of a wheel. Radiating out from my chest as far as one could see were lines or spokes. Starting from the same central point was another line, but this one swirled around clockwise and outwards. Connecting with each spoke. I felt myself expand outward to the left and right as far as possible. At each connection was a dot of light. This dot of light was me at a different point in time in a different existence. Just by looking at a certain dot of light, I could be there at will, instantly. The feeling of seeing myself in my true state is almost indescribable."*

Alexis, who was going through a stressful time in her life, floated out of her body as she was falling asleep. *"All of a sudden I found myself soaring and saw what looked like camp fires. As I approached each one, I remembered a different lifetime, each time flying higher and higher, realizing it was getting lighter and lighter. I went through at least seven different layers."*

THERE IS A REASON FOR EVERYTHING, EVEN SUFFERING

One teaching that runs through the experiences is that there is a divine purpose for everything that happens, even suffering. Jessica sought the reason we have to suffer and feels she now understands. Hear how other experiencers voice their new understanding.

Tory, who left his body during an intense desire to die, says, *"Everything is perfect! Nothing is 'wrong.' Even the greatest 'evil' to us in our limited thinking is the way it is meant to be."*

Thomas died at twenty-nine of a drug overdose. He states, *"Our purpose is to learn how to love others and how to receive love . . . I know everything happens for a reason, and for the ultimate good."*

Lydia, who was in an automobile accident, reports, *"I saw/experienced/recognized that everything that happens to us on earth is part of God's beautifully designed 'harmonious hologram.' Everything that happens here is ultimately so that our souls can experience love."*

LOVE IS THE PURPOSE OF LIFE

Jessica concludes that *"learning to love, sacrifice, and feel pain and loss"* are an important part of our learning here on earth. Other experiencers agree that our purpose on earth is to learn about love.

Candice, who left her body during a criminal attack, says, *"I . . . realize that our love for one another is the purpose of this life experience."*

Diane, whose blood pressure fell precipitously while she was preparing to give birth, shares: *"Helping people and expressing love at all times for each other is what we are here for."*

Kirk died of a drug overdose at age nineteen. He reports, *"I was told to tell souls to love one another."*

Patrik left his body for six hours at age thirty-four due to an allergic reaction to diagnostic dye, following a ruptured aneurysm. He says, *"When I asked about the ultimate goal I was told it was to develop the truest form of love. That form is, to make it simple to understand, when we get to the point that we would give up our time on the physical side to help another without thought of the consequences to ourselves."*

Jolie was in a coma five days at age twenty after her car crashed during a Maine snowstorm. She says, *"I think I came back to learn about what 'love' was. As a child I wondered because I didn't feel love or loved; I didn't know what it was. I wanted to know and in the coma I think I realized that love was one of those things that was both beautiful and also painful. Did I want to experience it? I did, because I didn't know what it was."*

Lydia, whose neck was broken during a terrible car accident, says, *"In the 'end,' love is the whole meaning, value, and purpose"* of our life here.

In the final chapter, we address the question, "What can I learn from near-death experiences about loving while I am still on earth?" In the eloquent introductory account, the experiencer learns about the importance of love here on earth. She and others help us better understand that, in all life, only love matters.

Chapter Nine

In Life, Love Is Most Important

> *The being of light showed me that all that was really important in life was the love we felt, the loving acts we performed, the loving words we spoke, the loving thoughts we held . . . And the love we'd felt during our lives was all that was left when everything else, everything perishable in life, had vanished.*
>
> – *Lynn*

After I experienced love pouring into me, I wanted to share that powerful love with everyone. However, I soon discovered that the love I received cannot be given as freely here on earth. I found it could be misinterpreted as romantic interest. I also had a greater desire to open my pocketbook and my home to others, but ran into questions about how and how much to do so. Giving love on earth is still sometimes challenging for me.

In our introductory experience, Lynn learns the importance of love in our lives here on earth. She also reports many of the same conclusions that others shared earlier in this book. Although her experience is longer, it is included in its entirety.

We will also hear from other experiencers who learn how to live better lives during their near-death experience, especially from their life review. Some specifically state that they receive reassurance and unconditional love following their life review, even when they have done seemingly unforgivable things. Some experiencers learn such things as the importance of treating everyone with love and kindness, of living life fully, and of choosing higher thoughts, emotions, and vibrations. Several talk about the challenges of loving after they return. Finally, more than a few say that love never ends.

LYNN'S EXPERIENCE

My near-death experience occurred when I was five years old, in Russia where I was born and lived at the time, on a holiday trip to the Black Sea where I went with my mother and grandparents. On this particular day we had all gone down to the beach.

The sea was rough, and my mother was standing in the water holding me in her arms. I remember feeling safe and secure, although the waves were huge, enormous from my five-year old perspective, and being excited as they came crashing over my mother and me, one by one.

Then this particularly big wave hit us, my mother lost her balance, lost her grip, and I was washed away by the wave. For a moment I felt the utter fear of death, my body instinctively sensing this being a life-threatening situation. I held my breath and struggled to find something to hold on to, to save myself, but my hands were only grasping water. Only water was everywhere, I was helpless, completely out of control.

Letting go

When I realized there was no use to fight, nothing to get a grip on, I surrendered. I let go of my breathing, let go of trying to save myself, let go of the struggle for life, and allowed whatever was happening to me to happen.

Next thing I remember is feeling the most profound and utter sense of peace I ever felt in my life. Suddenly I was feeling completely safe, being enveloped and protected by something I can only describe as complete unconditional love. This love was all around me, it was everywhere, but at the same time it was also me, the one I was, my innermost essence.

There was no longer any fear, no worries, no struggle for anything, and I could've gone on being wherever I was, and feeling the way I was forever. I felt as though I was finally being my true self. There were no limits or limitations whatsoever, I could go wherever I wanted, know whatever I wished, do anything. The sense of freedom was inexplicable. I was also strangely aware that the thing we ordinarily call 'time' now was suspended, and no longer existed.

Swept away into a world of love and light

Then I was swept away by some unknown force, and started to move at an enormous speed, which felt a lot faster than the speed of light. I traveled an enormous distance, literally traveled 'beyond the world.' I didn't have any sense of having a 'body,' just of moving like a thunderbolt through a darkness toward a point of brilliant light in the distance, and as I came closer to this light my only desire was to get to it, to get to where this light was.

When I reached the point of light I found myself in a world of light. Everything in this place was made of, and radiated light. It was beautiful and radiant beyond expression. 'Heaven' would be an adequate description, but I had no religious feeling, and knew there was no such thing as a 'hell.' I knew, without knowing how and why I knew this, that this was the place where everyone eventually got when they died, regardless of who they were and what they had done during their lives.

In the midst of the light stood a male figure. It was radiating this light, and radiating this totally unearthly complete unconditional Love. I was embraced by this being, or enveloped in its light, which felt like an embrace.

This was my home

Suddenly I remembered this place. This was my home, the place that was really my home, and I wondered how I could've ever forgotten about it. I felt as though, after a long, difficult journey in a foreign country, I finally had come home, and the being of light who was there before me was the being that knew me better than anyone else in creation. The being of light knew everything about me. It knew all I had ever thought, said or done, and it showed me my whole life in a flash of an instant.

I saw my life

I was shown all of the details in my life, the one I'd already lived, and all that was to come if I returned to earth. It was all there at the same time, all the details of all the cause and effect relations in my life, all that was good or negative, all of the effects my life on earth had had on others, and all of the effects the lives of others that had touched me had had on me.

Every single thought and feeling was there; nothing was missing. And I could experience the feelings and thoughts of all the other people involved, almost become them, which gave me pure experiential understanding of what brought other people pain, or joy, the positive or negative experiences, and effects of my own actions.

No judgment

The being was not judging me in any way during the life review, even though I saw a lot of shortcomings in my life. It simply showed my life the way it had been to me, and loved me unconditionally, which gave me the strength I needed to see it all, the way it was without any blinders, and let me decide for myself what was positive, negative, and what I needed to do about that. I don't remember any details of the events that were shown to me, neither past nor future, but I remember what was most important.

Love is most important

The being of light showed me that all that was really important in life was the love we felt, the loving acts we performed, the loving words we spoke, the loving thoughts we held. All that was made, said, done, or even thought without love was undone. It didn't matter. It simply didn't exist any longer. Love was all that was really important. Only love was real. Everything we did lovingly was as it was supposed to be. It was okay. It was good. And the love we'd felt during our lives was all that was left when everything else, everything perishable in life, had vanished.

Reunion

Next I remember finding myself in some other place, not knowing how I'd gotten there. The first being of light was gone, and I was surrounded by other beings, or people, who I felt as though I 'recognized.' These beings were like family, old friends, who'd been with me for an eternity. I can best describe them as my spiritual, or soul, family. Meeting these beings was like reuniting with the most important people in ones life, after a long separation. There was an explosion of love and joy on seeing each other again between us all.

Telepathic communication

The beings communicated with me, and one another in some kind of telepathic way. We spoke without words, directly, from mind to mind, or from spirit to spirit. None of us had any bodies. We were all made of some unknown substance, like a concentration of pure light; we were like dots of light in the light everywhere around us. Everybody knew what everybody else 'had in mind' instantly. There was no possibility, or need to hide anything from anybody. This kind of communication made misunderstandings impossible, and made us close in a way almost impossible to describe.

All are one

We were all individuals, but at the same time we were all one, united by indestructible bonds of love forever, and also united with the light in the world of light around us, being part of it, and part of each other's light.

The love these beings of light exuded healed me, swept away all the darkness in me, erased all of the pain and sorrow I'd accumulated during my life on earth. Earth and the life I'd lived on it felt very distant, was getting more distant all the time, almost like it had never really existed at all.

No time/no space

I was in this place with my soul family for a period of time that felt like an eternity. No 'time' in the usual sense existed here. Neither did the concept of 'space,' but even so there were different places to go, and spans of time that passed by. This is a contradiction in terms, but it is the only way I'm able to explain it in words. Spaceless space, timeless time. In this place there was only pure being. Except being 'healed' I don't remember what we did, just that we were together, and enjoyed it enormously.

I remember this 'world' of light as being huge, an enormous place, a place without limits or borders, neither individual nor external. I remember all beings who were in this place had complete, total knowledge, about all and everything. It was all pleasant, loving, beautiful beyond expression. Every 'thing' and 'being' in this place was made of light, and everything was light, even though there were individual 'things' and 'beings.' The light is what I remember best. It was living. Alive. A living light, that was everything and all, the essence of everything and all.

I had to go back

Next thing I remember is suddenly finding myself back in the presence of the being of light I'd met first, and told I had to go back. I said, "No way, I won't do it." This was about the last thing I wanted to do. Life on earth, filled with darkness, pain, sorrow, limits and limitations, was like a horrifying prison compared to this wonderful place, and I simply refused to go back. I was told that it wasn't my time, that I'd been granted a visit 'back home,' but that I had to fulfill my purpose and do the work I myself had chosen to do on earth.

Reminded of my purpose

The being of light reminded me that my purpose was to learn more about love, compassion, and how to express them on earth, and that my work was to help other people in any way I could. I had chosen this myself. And it told me that I would be back in the world of light in no time. "Never forget, in reality there is no time, only eternity itself," it said.

Next thing I knew I was back, feeling my body, the wave washed me up on shore again, and I was crawling up the shore coughing up a lot of seawater.

How the experience changed my life

As a child, I forgot my near-death experience, and the memory of it didn't return until many years later. Even so, it has always been with me and given me strength to cope with difficulties in my own life and to help and support others.

During the whole of my professional life I've been working with helping others in different ways. At the age of eighteen I started working with elderly people, dying, senile, physically and emotionally ill people. I worked with people with AIDS and the mentally ill. Later on I worked in the mental health care and social care area, among people with psychological, social, existential, emotional and spiritual difficulties, and always felt my work as being deeply meaningful, even before remembering my near-death experience. Currently I'm also working as a psychotherapist.

The near-death experience also put the foundation to my lifelong interest in the paranormal, the mystical, the unusual, and the spiritual, which I've had for as long as I can remember, not knowing why for many years.

After-effects

I've had after-effects in the form of 'paranormal' abilities and experiences, like having precognitive dreams and being able to sense, feel and see the true feelings and agendas of others, out-of-body and 'mystical' experiences, abilities and occurrences which have increased and decreased during the years, and sometimes given me problems, especially during the period when I didn't remember the experience, and didn't have any conscious understanding for why I had these abilities, what they were, and how they could be used.

The NDE led to, or at least I'm sure had something to do with, a profound spiritual emergence process I went through some years ago, a process that included profound changes in my understanding of life and world view, and involved Kundalini related experiences. The NDE has made me explore unknown dimensions, it has made me seek and find the answers to many questions, and to constantly strive to learn more about life, death, and everything in between, and to seek out ever new ways of helping others, which for me is the most meaningful thing one can do in life.

In the end, the near-death experience taught me as much about living as about dying, and constantly keeps on doing so.

Thank you, Lynn, for sharing this powerful experience. Now, let's look at various insights that Lynn and other experiencers brought back about how to live out of love.

To start with, we will look at lessons from Lynn's and others' life reviews. The life review is one of the most direct ways experiencers learn how best to live. They may also learn about love by interacting with a being on the other side, or they may simply return "knowing" new truths about love on earth.

IN OUR LIFE REVIEW, NO ONE JUDGES US BUT OURSELVES

Lynn speaks of the lack of judgment coming from the being who was with her during her life review. While not all report a life review, those who do often learn about the importance of love in earthly life. They often say they feel the feelings of others and have remorse about hurting others. No one reports being judged by anyone other than themselves, and those who judge themselves harshly receive reassurance.

WE MAY FEEL THE FEELINGS OF OTHERS

Lynn says she experienced "*the feelings and thoughts of all the other people involved,*" and that she could "*almost become them.*" This is one of the most striking points experiencers make about their life review: that they feel the feelings of those they affected, whether painful or pleasant, caused by their actions. An unusual aspect of Lynn's experience is that she not only felt the impact she had on others, but she realized how other people's lives had affected her as well.

Russell drowned while playing in a swimming pool when he was nine years old. *"I stood before the light and the light is God. God said to me, 'What have you done for me in your life?' I replied, 'I am only nine years old.' I was given a life review. Everything I had ever done or experienced up to that point was shown to me. I experienced everything from everyone else's point of view or emotions. Watching this life review was like watching a movie on a screen, but the screen filled my whole mind. When I was done I appeared back before God . . . The message I received from God is that God loves me and all the rest of the human race no matter who or what we are, race, color, etc."*

During his life review, Didier, who drowned during an accident at sea, recalls not only his own actions and feelings, but the feelings of others. Like Lynn, Didier had the unusual experience of being shown portions of his future life. *"While I was in the presence of these other beings, I experienced a life review. This was not just a review of what I had done in my life. I also experienced how my actions had affected and influenced other people, and further how their feelings and emotions were connected to my actions. It is hard to explain the intensities and details of the life review let alone the experiencing of all this without judgment. It was a feeling of growth and evolvement while I underwent this review. The review continued and I started seeing things that were unfamiliar to me, things that I had not yet lived or experienced . . . I then realized that I was seeing parts of my future."*

Dave was six years old when the truck in which he was riding with his parents and sister was involved in a terrible wreck and he was thrown through the windshield. A male being met Dave after he left his body and, in response to a question Dave asked, gave Dave some information about judgment. *"He said 'I have given each of you the gift of free will . . . I do not judge for I love everyone and forgive the unforgivable. This is a place of judgment. But each judges themselves. The wicked must know what it was like to be touched by them in their lives. To know what it was like to be their own victims.' He used much more technical words than this, but somehow I understood. And we never used spoken words. We communicated through thought."*

"I remember us talking about my abusive stepfather. Why it was allowed to continue. He simply said, 'Sometimes we are the victims of free will.' But to forgive those who have done you wrong, 'for in the end, vengeance is mine.'

"I understood what 'he' meant. Not that he would personally seek vengeance. But when each person passes away they are not alone. He is there with them, good or bad, walking at their side as they judge themselves. And what I found to be amazing was that 'he' never abandons those who have done wrong. For in the end, they must relive the pain and torture of their victims. Forgetting their hatred and anger that caused them to be the way they were. Instead, they too, in an ironic way, are victims of their own free will."

WE MAY FEEL REMORSE DURING OUR LIFE REVIEW

Lynn acknowledged that she saw shortcomings in her life during her life review, but the non-judgmental love of the being with her gave her strength *"to see it all, the way it was, without any blinders."* Most experiencers feel at least some remorse as their lives unfold before them. They explain, however, that they do not feel judged by anyone outside themselves.

Donny, who was eleven when he left his body while receiving anesthesia at the dentist's office, reported, *"I was put before 'God' without human defense mechanisms or denial. I had total realization of what I was and all that I had done on earth. I was naked before 'God.' The events I had done all carried full pain or joy without any buffer . . . In this place I felt all love, all acceptance, all forgiveness, all belonging, and reverence for the whole universe."*

Sorcha, who died in the automobile accident in New Zealand, states emphatically that we judge ourselves. *"WE ARE OUR OWN JUDGES WHEN IT COMES TO OUR LIFE REVIEWS . . . When we hurt another, intentionally or not, we suffer spiritual shame."*

Kathie, who died in the back seat of the moving car due to a heart condition, felt guilt during her life review. *"I came to a place, maybe a room, maybe a space. I was shown my life. If it was my entire life, I do not remember all of it. The only part that I remember now was just the last week or so. Since I had given up on God, I saw how selfish I had been. The things I had the most guilt for were hurting other people, lying, not being sensitive to their feelings, just being selfish. The fact that I was a lesbian didn't even seem to matter then. That was surprising to me, given what I had been brought up to believe."*

Harrison, who was being treated for the pulmonary embolism in a state prison, concluded after returning from the other side: *"Spiritual sin does not exist. Sin is a cultural concept which uses the fear of God's punishment to keep whole populations in line. It is impossible to sin spiritually as no soul would ever dream to cause harm to another soul. God is a God of love and does not punish."*

Tom was an addict and criminal who had a near-death experience, including a life review, after he tried to kill himself in jail. *"Then the movie-like panoramic screens began to pop up seemingly all around me, yet it was in my mind with me also. Hard to explain . . . So many people I had harmed. All of my dirty deeds, actions, and yes even my thoughts and things no one else could possibly know. It was all there around me, tormenting me. I felt all of their pain, all the torment I had caused to all.*

"Then the most horrible feelings of guilt, sorrow, and shame, and the like overcame me. I felt like someone forcing me to see the most horrible of things and would not let me turn away . . . What a miserable lost life I seen [sic] . . . Something in me was ratting me out, and it was myself, testifying against myself . . . I started thinking 'My God, what have I done.' This is judgment day and I am really going to a hell. When I heard myself saying things like that, it was like having another person inside my skin with me saying this stuff."

"I lost it, yelling out to God to take me out of here. I have seen enough, I yelled. Let me go. Then came the release. Even though I could not move still, a huge burdensome weight lifted from me, left me feeling just like a shell lying there. All I could feel at this point was absolute perfect love, and forgiveness. I was floating in an ocean of pure love and all power."

WE MAY RECEIVE REASSURANCE DURING OUR LIFE REVIEW

Although parts of Lynn's life review were painful for her to watch, she states that she was allowed to decide for herself what she wanted to change. No one said they were judged during their life review by anyone other than themselves. Many describe the reassurance they received in spite of the shame they felt while viewing their hurtful actions and words.

Walt, who was breathing the high-oxygen mixture while being treated for depression, briefly describes the reassurance he received. *"Following was an extensive life review which addressed hundreds of episodes and gave forgiving explanations all in a matter of seconds."*

Cecily was diagnosed with aplastic anemia after her first year of college and was waiting for a bone marrow transplant when she left her body and had a life review. *"Initially, I was filled with shame and remorse for every unkind thought and deed. I felt clearly all those occasions when I had the opportunity to show compassion and understanding, but instead was uncaring. I saw what great good I might have done and did not do. Let me tell you, looking at yourself through the eyes of everyone you've touched for better or worse is absolutely brutal; ten kindnesses cannot make up for feeling another's pain and knowing you were the cause. Inside I cried out, 'I'm sorry. I'm so sorry,' and a warm, loving humorous voice answered me, 'You're just a kid, how bad can you be?' This statement was accompanied by a gentle chuckle and a feeling of love and forgiveness so complete that it has never left me. I was enveloped in grace."*

Rowena, the thirty-five-year-old Jewish woman whose car hydroplaned and hit a pole in Australia, says this of the light being who accompanied her life review: *"He stood beside me and directed me to look to my left, where I was replaying my life's less complimentary moments. I relived those moments and felt not only what I had done but also the hurt I had caused, some of the things I never would have imagined could have caused pain. I was surprised that some things I may have worried about, like shoplifting a chocolate as a child, were not there whilst casual remarks which caused hurt unknown to me at the time were counted. When I became burdened with guilt I was directed to other events which gave joy to others. Although I felt unworthy it seemed the balance was in my favour. I received great Love."*

Avril, who left her body during a drug overdose when she was sixteen, says this of her life review: *"When it was all over with, I wished that my spirit would no longer exist. I hated myself. I was so sorry and hadn't realized how these things affected others. At that moment I saw a ray of light with a being in it and the love from his light filled my entire being up. It was like something I'd never experienced before and haven't experienced again to this day. I was crying and told him I was sorry. He asked why I had done these things, and I said that I had not remembered him. He said that I needed to make a choice, that I couldn't stay in the middle anymore. I said that there had never been a choice, that I loved him. At that moment he filled me with more love than I've ever known and my sins were forgiven of me . . . This spiritual being was someone I was very close with and loved. I was sorry that I had forgotten him after I came to earth."*

TREAT EVERYONE WITH LOVE AND KINDNESS

Lynn returned from her near-death experience knowing the importance of expressing love and compassion. She learned that helping others is the most meaningful thing in life. Many experiencers come back with an expanded understanding of love and how important it is to give it on earth. Once that higher dimension of love has permeated their consciousness, they want to bring it back and share it with others. We will look at some experiencers' insights about applying love in daily life.

Dino, who died from an allergic reaction, brought back some lessons from his life review. *"I experienced my life in review, things I had forgotten. The value in the acts of kindness with no agenda, the warmth toward others, how they felt, what other choices I could have made in some cases, and not with an idea of regret, but rather a noticing."*

Fiona, who almost drowned as a five-year-old child, speaks of what she learned. *"I have formulated and incorporated certain philosophies into my life. Every day I try to see the light of God in everyone I meet. I try to walk in the other person's shoes. I try to increase my capacity to love unconditionally. I treat others as I want to be treated. And last, but not least, I always remember that it's the little things that count, and it will be those little things that will stand out as your life flashes before your eyes."*

Lee, who was praying silently while awaiting a dental procedure when she left her body, tells how she shared the new understandings she brought back. *"The experience . . . has definitely opened my eyes to the goodness in all people. In fact, I am often jokingly teased by others that I never see the 'bad' in people and that I always have an 'excuse' for those who are behaving 'badly'. . . It's not that I don't see how people behave inappropriately at times, it's just that I know they have pain inside their souls and they don't know any other way to behave . . . I seem to have somehow become a type of role model for others when it comes to learning that we are all equal and should all be treated with love and compassion."*

Sorcha, who died in the automobile accident in New Zealand, shares her lesson. *"We must learn to forgive ourselves and others. It is not for us to bear a grudge or judge another . . . We can come to know, carry and share the light within us all, and that love/light is God's/Sacred Spirit's eternal unconditional Love and is accessible to all."*

Devin, who died in a vehicle accident, reports the main lesson he learned: *"I learned that the only thing to realize was that love and service was all there is to it! Nothing more nor less than just love and service. That's it."*

LIVE LIFE FULLY

Lynn concludes her account by saying that her near-death experience taught her as much about living as about dying. Others speak about learning the importance of living life fully.

Roberta was a young woman with lupus who almost died. From her near-death experience, she has learned how to live life out of love and now lives life more fully. *"I realized I had been living life in fear, fear of starting tasks because I probably would die from the Lupus, so why even get started? I have now learned to live life out of love. I don't fear death any more. Of course, I don't want to die, but I don't let that possibility keep me from interacting with others and starting big tasks. In fact, when I do die, I hope I am right in the big middle of something, using all my talents and gifts to their fullest, until God tells me I can quit now."*

Jet was a man of seventy who was dying of brain cancer when he had his near-death experience. *"I now believe our main obligation is to live life to its fullest and do it cleanly, within the guidelines of giving and caring . . . I can give a little of myself, give my love, and give prayer and help to others when I have the opportunity . . . help others through love, caring and understanding."*

Didier, who drowned during the accident at sea, discovered how it feels to live life fully. *"The two days after my near death . . . I was living with my heart wide open. I was experiencing everything through an open heart. When I say an open heart, I mean the light that you experience when in the presence of that unconditional love. That feeling of coming home is present in your heart, and your heart feels as though it has expanded beyond the physical body and is in touch with everything."*

Stella, who was eighteen when she overdosed, came back from her near-death experience able to live life more fully. *"If we only knew how much we're loved and how surrounded by it we are, all the false illusions of pain would simply melt away. So here I am – a 21-year-old kid who was sexually molested, emotionally abandoned, an avid atheist (because if there was a God, I had a big bone to pick with him) – and now am filled with the most optimistic joy and faith for not only myself, but that of all humanity!"*

Fiona, who almost drowned when she was five, learned to fear less and live more. *"I fear nothing. I learn as much as I can, live as much as I can live, and enjoy my every moment here, which is a gift."*

CHOOSE HIGHER EMOTIONS, THOUGHTS, VIBRATIONS

Lynn learned the value of loving feelings, acts, words, and thoughts from her near-death experience. Here are other statements experiencers made about the importance of overcoming negative emotions and thoughts and raising our vibrational level.

Berta had two in-depth near-death experiences, one during a SCUBA accident and another during a criminal attack when she suffered a fractured scull. She learned about emotions and their impact. *"With more knowledge, we no longer have the need to hate or be angry . . . We cannot allow our emotions to hold onto the negative light with sorrow any more than we need to hang onto an illness. All illness and sorrow are from the negative light. Our emotions are the motions of the spirit that move our soul . . . We must use our positive emotions to neutralize these sorrows and illnesses."*

Sorcha, who died in the automobile accident in New Zealand, learned about the power of thought. *"I saw how my thought alone had affected people in my life. The Power of Thought. Thoughts are powerful energy waves sent out, which are picked up and manifested into reality in some way, in the future . . . Thought forms have tremendous energy that is transmitted. That energy has power which affects those who transmitted it and those that receive it, as it ripples out on wave lengths to connect with similar forms and grows on the vibrational level that they belong to. Consequently, our thoughts affect the whole Universe."*

Sorcha also reported on the importance of raising our vibrational level. *"I was shown how we can change our vibrational levels. By changing the vibrational field that surrounds us, we are recreating our lives and creating miracles . . . Transformation/Healing can only take place when we don't allow doubt, fear and expectations to block the process but accept that God's will is done, not ours, by handing-up to our higher authority. I was shown how darker denser energy also has a path-hold in mankind; that healing is shared and spread around to eradicate all negative forms of denser energy. Mankind can play a conscious positive part in its own evolution. We are CO-creators and can unite heaven and earth by joining and integrating spirit into matter, manifesting in the now."*

SOME ENCOUNTER CHALLENGES AFTER COMING BACK

A major challenge Lynn faced after her near-death experience was understanding and dealing with her new abilities. A few experiencers report other types of challenges after returning from their experiences.

Didier, who drowned during the accident at sea, remembered the unconditional love and wanted to share it with others but learned it is not as easy here. *"By being able to touch the light, I was able to experience unconditional love. Because we are all human, our human self naturally puts conditions on our love. Whether it is the love for a girlfriend or a love for a snack, we have expectations. We expect love in return or at least certain behaviors. Unconditional love doesn't work that way. By living your life without expectations of others, by unconditionally giving your love, you build a true compassion that others can feel and are drawn to. But it also can cause trouble. The human side often misunderstands unconditional love. The human side creates expectations. It caused me some troubles before I recognized this fact."*

Davey, who died of starvation as a prisoner of war, realized that choosing peace is a challenge for all of humanity. *"Wars are always with us. At least I learned every one of us is responsible for them. If not directly, we acquiesce to them. Whether we can ever learn or desire enough not to war with one another is the big question."*

Tom, who had his near-death experience when he tried to kill himself in prison, encountered some challenges in bringing the love back into this life. During his experience, he had been instructed to come back and tell others how much God loves them. *"My first experience with a minister in there was awkward and very negative. First thing I was told by another human was that God would not use a person like me for something like that. And that God does not work like that nowadays to begin with. Besides I hadn't gone to a seminary."* Later, Tom shared with his counselors and didn't have any better reception from them. *"My old counselors put me on drugs (forced) for having an encounter like this."* In spite of these rebuffs, Tom says, *"I now loved and forgave everything and everybody. Even the cops. No rage, no shakes, no nothing . . . I was a new man . . . I am still clean and sober . . . This event changed me dramatically in every way you can think of."*

Quite a few experiencers report they are met with disbelief or ridicule when they first reveal what happened to them. Many wait a long time before talking about it at all, sometimes for fear of what others will think.

LOVE NEVER ENDS

Lynn learned that love is the only thing left when we go to the other side and that everything else in life is temporary. Others say there is an eternal love awaiting us all. We have heard most of the following statements before, but I repeat them here because they talk about the continuation of love beyond physical life or the eternal love that is always there for us all.

Cassandra, who drowned while innertubing in Texas, reported, *"When it is all over, none of the material things or petty differences count at all. The only thing you have to take with you is love."*

Jessica, the young woman who died during childbirth, said, *"The most important realization I came to is that the force of the universe is love, and that those who truly love will be with their loved ones forever."*

Cecilia, who almost died of the staph infection following childbirth, reported, *"And I do remember the one realization I had as I ascended through the heavens was that you only take one thing with you as you pass from this existence, 'LOVE.'"*

Debrah was twenty-eight when she left her body after receiving anesthesia prior to surgery. She spent the entire operation in a beautiful meadow, walking and talking with others, before returning. She states definitively, *"There is no death and there is no end to love."*

Donny, the eleven-year-old who had a near-death experience after the dentist put him under anesthesia, said, *"I know there is hope for an eternal existence in love, peace, and joy."*

Sorcha, who died in the car crash in New Zealand, spoke of eternal love: *"There are no words to describe the . . . eternal energy of love and pure acceptance."*

Tabitha, who had the near-death-like dream of being with Mother Mary, said, *"I woke up 'knowing' that God's love is infinite and eternal and unconditional FOR EVERY ONE OF US."*

We have now heard from more than a hundred experiencers about their encounters with the world of love and light. Many have spoken eloquently of their new understandings about love, which they brought back with them. Without their courage and willingness to share with others, this enlightening, encouraging information would not have been available to us. We honor each experiencer and we thank them for bringing these new insights back to share with us. This is just a beginning, not the end. There is much more to learn.

AFTERWORD

My journey of self-discovery continues. Before I learned of my own near-death experience, I wanted to know what it was like to visit heaven, as so many of my friends from IANDS who had near-death experiences have done. I signed up for a between-lives regression by Michael Newton, author of *Journey of Souls*.[10]

During that regression, I experienced an awesome hug from my most powerful guide when I first arrived in the light: we walked towards each other until our orbs merged. We absorbed each other's energy and I felt his great wisdom. I recognized everyone there by their energy rather than by appearance, since we all looked like orbs of light. I also met with my family soul group and with another soul group made up of women ministers, some of whom I know in this life. The ministers were all golden orbs like me, and we were overjoyed to see each other. The last person I met was Jesus. He looked like his historical self, with a flowing robe. I fell to my knees before him in reverence and felt his great love for me.

Just two years ago, I received a strange telephone call from a woman who had attended a few sessions of my "Near-Death and Other Mystical Experiences" group in Tulsa, Oklahoma. She told me she had received some information about me from spirit that I might be interested in. I was curious, so she went on to inform me I had drowned when I was two and wasn't revived until I had been taken to a hospital in an ambulance.

This was before I had any memories of that momentous event in my life, and that was all she could tell me about it. I had no idea how I could verify the accuracy of her incredible assertion since my parents, aunts and uncles had all passed on. I called my two older cousins, but they hadn't heard of such a thing.

When I mentioned it to a friend from IANDS, she suggested I find someone who could regress me and see if I could retrieve any memories of it. Shortly after that, I found a regression therapist and gave it a try.

I relaxed with my eyes closed on the therapist's massage table. When she asked me what I saw in my mind's eye, I became anxious. I said my fingers were slipping off of my father's bare shoulder. I tried to hang on, but I couldn't. After that, the experience unfolded steadily as I went from one image to the next, just as recounted in Chapter One. I found myself sobbing at the end. I couldn't ever remember feeling so loved.

That was the first time I remembered my own near-death experience. It explained so many things about my life. My fear of getting my head under water while swimming. My joy as

I sang "I love to tell the story of unseen things above" as a child in Vacation Bible School. My fascination with near-death experiences and my need to know more about them.

Later, I went to another regression therapist to find out more about the circumstances surrounding my drowning. From that regression I recalled that my family was on a picnic in a park at Great Falls, Virginia, along the Potomac River, not far from where I grew up in Arlington, Virginia. The pictures I saw and the feelings I had during both these regressions, as well as the explanations they provided for so many things in my life, convinced me I really had drowned.

I am now certified in past life regression therapy myself. I am honored to help others discover past-life sources of issues in their lives and to resolve them. I also perform weddings and funerals, and I continue to volunteer from time to time as a hospice chaplain. Whenever I attend funerals, I try to share a few healing words with the bereaved, reminding them that their loved one is happy and free and will always love them (and not only forgives them, but understands them now).

I believe this book is part of the purpose I chose before coming here. I hope these accounts will lead you, as they have me, to more love and to a greater understanding of how very much you are cherished and loved for exactly who you are.

NOTES

1. Raymond A. Moody, Jr., M.D., *Life After Life: The Investigation of a Phenomenon – Survival of Bodily Death* (New York: Bantam Books, 1976; first published by Mockingbird Books, Covington, GA, 1975).

2. Elisabeth Kübler-Ross, M.D. *On Death and Dying: What the dying have to teach doctors, nurses, clergy and their own families* (New York: Macmillan Publishing Company, 1969).

3. The International Association for Near-Death Studies (IANDS) is headquartered at 2741 Campus Walk Avenue, Building 500, Durham, NC 27705-8878 and may be reached online at www.iands.org or by phone at 919-383-7940.

4. A few researchers did focus on love. Charles Flynn addressed the love encountered by NDErs (Charles P. Flynn, *After the Beyond: Human Transformation and the Near-Death Experience* (New York: Prentice Hall Press, 1986)). Kenneth Ring and Evelyn Elsaesser Valarino address love in *Lessons from the Light* (Kenneth Ring and Evelyn Elsaesser Valarino, *Lessons from the Light: What We Can Learn from the Near-Death Experience* (Portsmouth, NH: Moment Point Press, 1998)). Dr. Pam Kircher entitled her book about near-death experiences, including her own, *Love is the Link* (Pamela M. Kircher, M.D., *Love is the Link: A Hospice Doctor Shares Her Experience of Near-Death and Dying* (Burdett, NY: Larson Publications, 1995)).

5. The permission statement signed by those who submitted their account to IANDS says: "I wish the account of my experience to be placed in the IANDS archives. I understand that it will be coded for anonymity and may be read by students or researchers who have been approved in accordance with

IANDS' policies for use of the archives. My account may be excerpted or used in full, or data may be drawn from it in conjunction with any responsible study or project, including but not limited to classroom presentations, lectures or educational programs on near-death studies, or presentations at a professional conference; or as part of an academic paper, thesis or dissertation; or as part of an article for a professional journal or other responsible periodical, or in a book. My name will not be used unless I give express written permission to do so." Although all gave permission for their account to be published and most gave permission for their name to be used, I only use the pseudonyms assigned unless I have been able to contact the submitter personally and obtain explicit permission.

6. Jeffrey Long, M.D. with Paul Perry, *Evidence of the Afterlife: The Science of Near-Death Experiences* (New York: Harper One, 2010).

7. Guillain-Barré syndrome (GBS) is a rare disorder in which the person's own immune system damages the nerve cells, causing muscle weakness and sometimes paralysis. In rare cases, people have died of GBS, usually from difficulty with breathing. [www.cdc.gov accessed March 24, 2011]

8. The "silver cord" that Dawn refers to has been reported as connecting the physical and spirit bodies while the spirit is outside the body. It enables the spirit to return to the body. If the final decision is made by the soul to stay on the other side, the silver cord is severed. The silver cord is mentioned in various texts including the Biblical passage in Ecclesiastes 12:6: "Remember your creator in the days of your youth, before the days of trouble come . . . because all must go to their eternal home, and the mourners will go about the streets; before the

silver cord is snapped, and the golden bowl is broken . . . and the dust returns to the earth as it was, and the breath returns to God who gave it." (RSV)

9. "Shared-death experience" is a term used by Raymond Moody, Jr., M.D. in his book *Glimpses of Eternity: Sharing a Loved One's Passage from this Life to the Next* (with Paul Perry (New York: Guideposts, 2010)). A shared-death experience occurs when a healthy person's consciousness accompanies a dying person's spirit for a time as they move toward the world of love and light. At some point, the healthy person returns, and the dying person continues on into the light.

10. Michael Newton, *Journey of Souls: Case Studies of Life Between Lives* (Woodbury, MN: Llewellyn Publications, 1994).

ACKNOWLEDGMENTS

First, I wish to acknowledge the International Association for Near-Death Studies (IANDS) for collecting and making available to me the many accounts I received for my research. I also wish to make clear that the conclusions I have drawn are my own and do not necessarily reflect those of IANDS, its Board, or its members.

I also want to thank all my beloved friends and relatives for giving me love during this life on earth.

I want to thank those who helped me learn about near-death experiences, especially Elisabeth Kübler-Ross. The IANDS organization has provided wonderful conferences and its members and other attendees have shared their hearts and souls with me and welcomed me with open arms, especially Dr. Pam Kircher, Martha Cassandra St. Claire, Linda Jacquin, Jan Holden, Kim Clark Sharp, Beverly Brodsky, and many others.

I want to thank the faculty, students, and residents at Sancta Sophia Seminary for surrounding me with love during my seven years as a student there, especially Betty Carper, Sally Brown, Grace Bradley, Cedar Carrier, Lucille Perry, and many others.

I want to thank my friends at the Tulsa Near-Death and Other Mystical Experiences group who have helped me keep this IANDS-affiliated group going for seven years, especially Linda Goodwin, Eloise Crowley, Bob Boots, Barbara Lenihan, Ruth Ann Odom, Sherry Thurman, and many others.

I especially want to thank Lee Warren, my talented and loyal editor, who edited my doctoral dissertation and has worked with me many long hours to prepare this manuscript for a larger audience. She has been fun to work with, patient, sensitive, kind, grounded, generous, and wise. Thank you, Lee, for making this book possible.

I want to thank my children, John and Ben Houghton, for choosing me as their mother. My daughters-in-law, Laura and Kay, and my grandchildren, Jonathan, Robby, Trevor, Janel, Darby and Cale, are also precious to me. My sister Lynn Ellis is a valuable friend.

Long-time friends, Mary Power Garlock, Rita Shore, Dreama Frisk, and Charla McMillan Lowery have been a comfort in this life.

Finally, to all those whose accounts I have read and quoted, you have taught me more about life and love than I have found anywhere else. I am grateful that you wrote your story down for those of us who are seeking a higher truth.

INDEX

INDEX OF NARRATIVE ACCOUNTS

ABOUT THE AUTHOR

Ann Frances Ellis retired from her first career as a computer programmer, database researcher, and data communications network manager and later served as a hospice and hospital chaplain. She enjoys researching her Choctaw heritage and lives in Tulsa, Oklahoma with her rat terriers, Mattie and Lillie.